THE CHALLENGE OF THE MIND

RYUHO OKAWA

IRH PRESS

THE CHALLENGE OF THE MIND

AN ESSENTIAL GUIDE *to* BUDDHA'S TEACHINGS: ZEN, KARMA, and ENLIGHTENMENT

RYUHO OKAWA

Published under the same title in
Great Britain in 2004 by Time Warner Book Group UK.

Originally published in Japan as
Kokoro No Chousen -Syukyo No Kanousei Towa Nanika-
in 1994 by IRH Press Co., Ltd.

BOOKS
IRH PRESS
New York

Library of Congress Cataloging-in-Publication Data

ISBN 13: 978-1-942125-45-7
ISBN 10: 1-942125-45-3

First Edition
Second Printing

Printed in India
Cover Designer: Whitney Cookman

CONTENTS

TWO

WHAT IS BUDDHA-NATURE?

THREE

THE ESSENCE OF ZEN MEDITATION

FOUR

TRANSCENDENTAL WISDOM AND FORGIVING LOVE

FIVE

THE BENEFITS OF AN EGOLESS PERSPECTIVE

SIX

PRACTICING THE PHILOSOPHY OF THE MIDDLE WAY

SEVEN

ENLIGHTENMENT AND SPIRITUAL POWERS

EIGHT

WHAT IS KARMA?

PREFACE

This book will serve as an excellent guide for those who are longing for the mystical world of religion and seeking a Buddhist perspective as they go through their life's journey. We have entered a new religious age. Now is the time for us at Happy Science to prove that true religion can be compatible with a highly intellectualized society. In these times, ardently reading this book is proof that you are, in this sense, a real intellectual.

True religion teaches the challenge and potential of your mind. Its teachings represent the spirit of the Buddha and the essence of religion. This book invites you to explore the infinite heights of a wisdom appropriate to our times. When you understand that practicing religion is synonymous with becoming the forerunner of a new era, you will have reached a higher perspective from which to look out over a whole new world. Together let us take on the challenge of the mind!

Ryuho Okawa
Founder & CEO
Happy Science Group

ONE

THE LAW OF CAUSE AND EFFECT

1

Perspectives from Different Religions: Are Humans Separate from God or Integrated with God?

In this chapter, I would like to offer a general, introductory discussion of the law of cause and effect. This idea is very important, because it is closely connected to the principle of taking responsibility for oneself, which is something our organization, Happy Science, emphasizes greatly.

Before proceeding to the main topic, I would like to look at the different types of religions. Religions around the world can be divided into two broad categories. One type of religion isolates humans from God. These religions describe God and human beings as completely separate from one another and as completely different kinds of beings. Christianity is a typical example of this sort of religion. According to Christian doctrine, humans can have faith in God as the object of worship, but they cannot become God, nor does God become human. Although Jesus Christ is said to be the Son of God and to have acted as a bridge between God and human beings, God and human beings are definitely classified as separate from each other. This view of separating humans from

God is at the basis of faith in the other-power or a power outside oneself.

The other type of religion integrates human beings with God. These religions hold that human beings can become one with God. They espouse the idea that human beings can come close to God or become like God because humans possess the same divine nature within themselves. To put it simply, this means that human beings and God essentially share the same nature. So although humans can sometimes become deluded or corrupted by the things of this world and at times may even commit sinful acts, by removing these impurities and continuing to refine themselves spiritually, they can become one with God and even elevate themselves to become Godlike beings. Buddhism is often said to be an exemplar of this type of religion, which inevitably focuses on self-power.

So there are two basic types of religion: religions that isolate humans from God and teach salvation by faith alone, and religions that integrate humans with God and focus on self-power. By distinguishing these two types, however, I do not mean that one is right and the other wrong. Religions that isolate humans from God regard humans as weak and God as possessing enormous power. The idea is that, before a colossal God, tiny human beings should be humble, throwing themselves on the mercy of other-power so that they might live better lives by correcting their minds and hearts. In this type of religion, people become humble and pray to God. They also develop deep gratitude and intend to live with God's blessing—and this itself is a right attitude. These religions, however, tend to take the view that human nature is essentially evil. They are inclined to maintain that human beings are basically sinful and that only by the grace of God can there be forgiveness.

In contrast, religions that integrate human beings with God are fundamentally strong in the sense that they affirm that humans can come close to God. In other words, a firm belief that human nature is essentially good lies at the basis of these religions. Because human beings have the same precious nature as God, they have the potential to become like God. But in this three-dimensional physical world, their essential nature often becomes obscured, which can become problematic. So the main focus of our spiritual training here on earth is learning how to be free from the bondage and delusions of the third-dimensional world.

Both these types of religions offer right perspectives, but for my part, I attach greater importance to the idea that human beings have been gifted with a wonderful innate nature that they can cultivate through their own efforts. The reason I feel this way is that when we depend on other-power, we can't expect much development from humanity. Of course, I understand the feeling of wanting to escape present suffering and seek salvation from an outside power as quickly as possible, but once this desire has been fulfilled, we often stop right there. When we are saved, feel grateful to God, and attain happiness for the time being, we tend to feel satisfied and make no further progress.

In religions that teach integration of humans with God, on the other hand, there is an infinite path that opens before us, a path that leads to boundless progress and development. If we consider that human beings are souls who reincarnate into this three-dimensional world again and again for spiritual training, which of the two will do more good in the end? Which type do you think will lead as many people as possible to the other shore—the shore of true happiness? When I compare these two types of religion—one that expects human beings to plead for forgiveness each time they reincarnate, saying, "God, please forgive my sins for I am a sinner" and one that teaches people to think about how they can achieve a higher level of enlightenment step by step by refining and developing their souls every time they are born into this world—all in all, I recommend the latter type: religions that teach self-power.

Some people have become so corrupt that there seems to be very little possibility of their developing self-power, but deep down even these people still have faint aspirations to enlightenment. In such cases, religions that focus on salvation from other-power can give them an incentive to lead a better life. In Buddhism, this concept of other-power emerged in what was called the Pure Land Buddhism.*

* Pure Land Buddhism is one of the most popular traditions of Buddhism in East Asia and focuses on faith in Buddha Amitabha ("Buddha of Infinite Light").

2
The Basis of Buddhism:
Equality and Fairness

As I've just explained, Buddhism teaches the integration of human beings with God. Our organization, Happy Science, is based on the spirit of Buddhism and so places more emphasis on this idea than on the idea of a separation between humans and God. And this is evidenced by the fact that we uphold the idea that every human being has the same divine nature as Buddha.

Of course, we may need to consider the difference between God and Buddha here.* To put it simply, in Buddhism a "buddha" is someone who has experienced a human life on Earth and returned to the other world to live there as a high spirit with divine powers. This means that a human being can become divine, and this is the basis of the type of religion that teaches integration of human beings with God.

To achieve this union, a human being must undergo a great deal of spiritual discipline in this world, including

---

* I have offered a detailed explanation of this topic in the final chapter of *The Challenge of Religion*. The original Japanese title of this book is *Shuukyou No Chousen* (Tokyo: IRH Press, 1993). This title is currently unavailable in English.

guiding and saving many others. Only after doing this can a person return to the other world as a high spirit with exactly the same powers as Buddha. In Japan, there is a customary idea that everyone will automatically become a buddha at the time of death, but this is utterly wrong. The truth is that we can only become a buddha after we've accomplished a great task and become worthy.

In religions that isolate humans from God, human beings can never become God, no matter how hard they try to perfect themselves. God is an entirely separate being, for He is the Creator of human beings, while human beings are the creatures or created beings. In Judeo-Christian religions, you find the idea that God created human beings by gathering and mixing clay or dust or by breathing life into pieces of broken rib.

If there is a clear distinction between the Creator and the created, then the created can never become the Creator. There is even the allegory that humans were driven out of paradise when they attempted to become like the Creator by taking forbidden fruit in the Garden of Eden. In short, the fact that Eve was tempted by the serpent in the Garden of Eden to eat the fruit of the tree of knowledge signifies that humans tried to become omniscient and omnipotent like God, but in vain. So here we see a clear distinction between God and human beings; this story represents the idea that God becomes angry when humans attempt to overstep the line dividing them from God.

We can find a similar idea in the story of the Tower of Babel. When human beings built a very high tower in an effort to reach the kingdom of God, or heaven, God became wrathful, and the people suffered a great disaster: they could no longer understand one another's words. This story makes clear the idea that God is fundamentally different from human beings.

If you study the concept of the multidimensional world that I teach at Happy Science, you will see that gods and human beings are different because they belong to different dimensions. But they are also fundamentally the same in the sense that they share the same innate nature. So they are different in terms of their degree of spiritual evolution, or the amount of spiritual light they emit. The inner self of every human being is like a diamond, but it will shine more brilliantly depending on how much it is polished—that is, how much care it receives. Just as diamonds are graded, people settle in different dimensions in the other world depending on how polished their souls are. By polishing their inner selves, people can rise to higher dimensions, beginning in the fourth dimension and moving through the fifth, sixth, seventh, and eighth to the ninth dimension.

The dimension the soul goes to in the other world corresponds precisely to the level of enlightenment that the person has achieved in this world. Someone who emits a great spiritual light in this world will return to the corresponding world in the beyond. A person who has attained a seventh-dimension level of enlightenment in this world will return to the world in the seventh dimension, and someone with a fifth-dimensional level of enlightenment will return to the world in the fifth dimension. So, how much a soul shines in this world corresponds exactly to where it will go in the other world. This is the Buddhist idea.

Accordingly, we can view human beings as having an innate potential to evolve, and in this respect, everyone is equal. However, in the process of numerous reincarnations over a long period of time, substantial differences have developed among souls. And based on a fair judgment of the outcome of each life, some souls have evolved while others have not. This does not change the fact that we all have the potential to evolve, no matter what era we live in—even now. This latent potential shines forth when it comes into contact with the dharma (Buddha's Truths), which acts as a catalyst that gives us an opportunity to increase our level of enlightenment. This idea is at the core of my teachings on the spiritual training we undergo.

3
Causality Is the Law of the Great Universe

Now let's look in detail at the main topic of this chapter: causality. The idea is that everything has a cause and an effect, and the world unfolds in chains of cause and effect.

Let me give you an example. When molecules of hydrogen and oxygen are heated, a chemical reaction occurs, resulting in small drops of water. When a large quantity of these drops is collected, water is produced. When a large amount of water is collected, a pond, a river, or an ocean forms. An ocean provides an environment that gives rise to marine life and allows sea creatures to live, which allows other forms of life that feed on them appear. Or take minerals, for instance. They are made up of crystals that are formed through chemical reactions. Plants also require certain conditions to grow; first of all, of course, there must be a seed, and then there need to be certain nutrients in the soil. When rain falls and the sun shines, plants grow quickly. Around them are herbivorous animals that feed on them; human beings and other creatures also live on them.

As I have just illustrated, first there is the cause, or the combining of one element with another, which gives rise to a new result; this result, in turn, becomes the cause that produces another new result. When we view the world in this way, we see that everything is produced by chains of cause and effect.

For humans, the same idea holds true. First, there is a mother and a father; then a child is born. That child then marries the child of another family, and a new child is born. In this way, long, uninterrupted family lineages have allowed human history to continue for tens of millions of years or more. Without such chains of cause and effect, human beings would not exist today. The teachings of Shakyamuni Buddha, too, have been passed down to us through 2,600 years simply because humankind has continued to this day. If human beings had died out completely in the time of Shakyamuni, his teachings would not have remained. Everything works in this way.

Here we become aware of an interesting fact. The world is formed according to the law of cause and effect, or the law of causality, and human beings can improve themselves and become higher beings depending on the choices they make within the circumstances of this world while undergoing spiritual training. As they advance, they are led to walk the path to Buddha.

In fact, the idea of cause and effect is exactly the same as the law of the great universe. In other words, the universe operates under one law, or one rule. Everything unfolds according to this law. Earth and all the stars, nebulae, and solar systems are subject to this one law. In three-dimensional space, too, all things operate according to the law of causality.

As I've mentioned, there are also chains of cause and effect in the vertical flow of time. There are chains of parents and children, children and grandchildren, grandchildren and great-grandchildren. Plants, too, bear fruit each year, and this, in turn, generates the next link in the chain of life. In autumn there is the harvest. At that time, the seeds fall to the ground or are sown by human hands, and the following year they grow. Again, they bear fruit in autumn, and again seeds fall. Similarly, the leaves on the trees bud in spring, grow thick in summer, turn red in autumn, and finally shrivel and fall in winter.

Spatially and temporally, all things arise from the chains of cause and effect. These chains do not exist independently of one another, but are intertwined in complicated ways, bringing time and space into existence. That is what is meant by the idea that this world is created by the law of cause and effect.

4
The Power of Reason Underlies the Law of Causality

The law of causality is the law of the universe; this is the principle of Buddha's ideas. So the law can also be regarded as Buddha's ideal, Buddha's will, or even the life of Buddha itself.* In fact, Buddha is the law, and this world was created based on this law.

In Christianity, there is a clear distinction between the Creator and the created. In Buddhism, however, this figurative explanation of the creation of the world is replaced by the idea that everything operates under the law. This law could be termed "the will of Buddha," "the ideal of Buddha," or "the power of Buddha." In other words, Buddha let this universe unfold under a single law. Buddhism teaches that all things and all phenomena, including human beings, are subject to this law and that this law is Buddha Himself.

Shakyamuni Buddha taught that those who see the chains of cause and effect see dharma, and those who see

---

* Here, Buddha means the Primordial Buddha, which is equivalent to the Creator.

dharma see how everything unfolds through cause and effect. So dharma is essentially the law of causality.

The word "dharma" has several meanings. First, it refers to the teachings. The law of the universe, or Buddha's dharma, in fact, teaches us what causality is, so if you can fully understand causality, you will understand dharma. Another meaning of dharma is the existence of all creation. So, when Shakyamuni Buddha taught that those who see dharma would discover the law of cause and effect, he meant that they would see this law operating in all living things and in all the phenomena of this universe.

This means that nothing in this world exists without a cause. Consider an everyday item such as your shirt, your desk, or your watch. First came the raw materials, which were processed by human hands before the end product came into existence. Each item began with an intention to produce it. All things in this world are created by chains of cause and effect, often by the hands of many. Everything has a cause, and why and how it came to exist can be explained by the law of causality.

When Shakyamuni Buddha taught that those who see dharma see the law of causality and those who see the law of causality see dharma, he meant that dharma, both in the sense of the teachings and in the sense of existence, is based on chains of cause and effect. But if we explain the physical makeup of material objects solely based on this idea of causality, Buddhist ideas may be mistaken as materialistic. We should be very careful not to make this mistake.

Shakyamuni's causal explanation for the existence of all things shows that he had a logical perspective and a rational understanding of all things. In other words, this explanation itself is a reflection of the vast power of reason that Shakyamuni Buddha embodied. The power of reason, which has had a great influence on various fields of academic study, such as medicine and the natural sciences, is also inherent in Buddhism. Buddhism is therefore quite different from religions that merely promise their followers certain benefits and the dubious new religions that have become prevalent today. In Buddhism, there is a very rational and logical way of thinking, a scientific approach. If you understand the idea of cause and effect, you will see this clearly.

5
Applying the Idea of Causality to Spiritual Training in Life:
The Principle of Self-Responsibility

In the previous section, I said that the idea of causality can explain the existence of all things. I also said that dharma, when it is interpreted as the teachings, means the law of cause and effect, and vice versa. Simply put, the teachings explain the chains of cause and effect. Let me explain what this means.

In reality, human beings are surrounded by two worlds, this three-dimensional world and the other world. This latter world is the original home of human beings and so is also called "the real world." Occasionally we reincarnate into this physical world to undergo spiritual training, and then we return to the other world. As we go through this cycle of birth, death, and rebirth, our lives are subject to this law of cause and effect. And the teachings explain that this law of causality is at work throughout our lives.

No one can escape this law. The harvest we reap depends on how we have tended the seeds we have sown.

The seeds are the causes, and how we have tended them are the conditions. Our harvest is the results we achieve.

We are born and grow up in different sets of conditions, and as a result of the way we live, we return to different places in the other world. Some even go to hell. There are innumerable realms in hell. In fact, there are as many hells as the number of nightmares that human beings can have.* In the course of your life, you've probably had many nightmares, but there are actually many, many more kinds of hell than the number of bad dreams you've had, more than the total number of all your friends' bad dreams put together, so there are not just one or two hundred hells, but thousands and tens of thousands. There are as many realms in hell as the number of wrong ways of thinking in this world. If a person's way of thinking is wrong and it is a way of thinking that no one else shares, that person can create a hell of his own. If the same sort of people gather, they create their own shared hell. Everything is subject to this rule.

In the Buddhist worldview, there is no fearsome God who drives people to hell as punishment or takes others up to heaven. Instead, everything operates according to certain laws. And these laws apply to every soul. So it

---

* The universe is multidimensional, and the world we inhabit is in the third dimension, which consists of three elements: length, width, and height. While heaven stretches from the fifth to the ninth dimensions, hell occupies only a tiny section of the fourth dimension. Those in hell have the chance to return to heaven through self-reflection and repentance. See *The Laws of Eternity* (New York: IRH Press, 2024) for more information about the multidimensional structure of the spirit world.

is clear what kinds of experiences will lead us closer to Buddha and what kinds of experiences will lead us toward darkness.

While we live under these laws, we can use our free will to make certain choices throughout the decades of our present lifetime. Human beings are given complete freedom in our choices. Of course, as living creatures on Earth, we human beings cannot survive without certain basic necessities, and we cannot be completely free from relationships with other people. But within these parameters, we are able to think and act freely. For example, anyone can kill a person if they really want to. But most people do not kill others even if they feel an urge to, because they restrain themselves, thinking it's wrong to do so. Some may not know the exact reason why they refrain from doing so, but at least they know that such acts should not be done or that if they do them, they will face consequences. This is because people have the knowledge of good and evil, which they have learned over the course of numerous incarnations, and this knowledge has become wisdom that has penetrated deep into the soul. Not everyone is aware of this wisdom early in life, but as they listen to others and learn from books, they learn to behave correctly. They can do so because a considerable amount of knowledge is in fact already accumulated in their souls. They awaken to this knowledge when something outside themselves brings it to their attention.

If, on the other hand, human beings came into existence by accident, like crane flies that appear at a pond on a sunny day, then each time we were born, we would have to decide all over again what good and evil are; otherwise we'd have no way of dealing with various situations. But in fact, we already have this knowledge to a certain extent from our experiences in past incarnations. We possess about 80 percent of this knowledge innately and acquire the remaining 20 percent while undergoing spiritual training in our present lifetime. We will be held responsible for what we have chosen in this life and also in our next incarnation. This is the idea of causality applied to spiritual training; no one can escape this law.

6
The Law of Causality Is the Essence of Buddhism

As I've explained, the chain of cause and effect can be applied spatially as well as temporally. The law of causality is in fact equivalent to the idea of the absolute God in the religions that isolate humans from God. This idea is by no means atheism or materialism; it is in fact a remarkable teaching that expounds the law that rules the universe. Shakyamuni discovered this law and lived within the law in the best way possible for a human being, and that is why he continues to exist as the Buddha even after his return to heaven and is considered the highest spiritual entity.

The soul contains a divine nature, and if you perceive the law of the universe and lead the best possible life in accordance with the law, you can become a divine being of the highest spiritual level; this is the teaching of Buddhism. So when the Buddha appeared, representing the highest human ideals, traditional gods could no longer be regarded as beings of an even higher order. The truth is that the traditional gods are high spirits who incarnated on Earth in times past, but the Buddha emerged as a being that surpassed them.

Even the Buddha cannot alter the law of the universe, but he embodies this law and manifests it at the highest level. What's more, Buddhism teaches that anyone can become a buddha through continual spiritual training, though it may take many, many years. This is what is great about Buddhism; the dharma gate is open to everyone.

But at the same time, it is essential to know that the results of your life will be judged fairly and precisely. Some people believe that all they have to do to find salvations is believe, but this simple teaching does not represent the essence of Buddhism. For instance, some say that you will be saved if you chant the mantra that reveres Amida Buddha, worship an image of the Buddha, venerate a hanging scroll, or just sit in meditation. Others say that a board mandala will bring happiness to your life. Today, there are numerous sects that call themselves Buddhist, but their teachings are a long way from the true teachings of the Buddha.

The Buddha's teaching can be summed up in the following way: All things arise through chains of cause and effect. Perceive the chain, and endeavor to improve it. If you do this, you can save yourself. Who is the one who can save herself? She is a god. This means that divine beings and human beings are not completely separate: the ones who save and the ones who are saved are integrated. Humans can actually save themselves, which is synonymous with achieving divinity. So human beings can become divine.

By learning and mastering the laws, we can save ourselves; in other words, we can become divine spirits. This is the big difference between Buddhism and religions that isolate humans from God. There are other, more detailed discussions of the law of causality that I can offer, but for now, I will be glad if you can understand the fundamental basis of the law of causality that I have discussed in this chapter.

TWO

WHAT IS BUDDHA-NATURE?

1

Our Inner Potential and Condition for Attaining Enlightenment

In this chapter, I would like to talk about the teaching of Buddha-nature. Buddha-nature literally refers to the nature of Buddha within us and comes from the concept of a buddha, which is any person who has achieved or holds the ability to achieve enlightenment. Buddha-nature, then, is essentially our capacity for enlightenment. So, since Buddha-nature exists in everyone, all of us possess within ourselves the means to attain buddhahood. To put it another way, Buddha-nature is the inner potential for enlightenment that resides in everyone.

However, as I also have said in *The Challenge of Enlightenment**, we need to keep one thing in mind: the potential for enlightenment is simply a potential; it is not the same as a result. This is a very important point we must remember. The fact that we each hold the potential to become a buddha, the inner nature that leads to enlightenment, does not necessarily mean that everyone

* See Ryuho Okawa, *The Challenge of Enlightenment* (New York: IRH Press, 2022).

will be able to attain buddhahood. It's worth noting that you have to go through the proper course that will lead you to this final goal.

All sorts of religions are being practiced around the world, and I have been concerned to see many new, eccentric religions in Japan that tend to overlook the law of cause and effect. I find this troubling, because these religions don't have a logical basis to explain how their teachings will lead you to enlightenment. Meanwhile, I have also seen that many traditional religions have become ossified and reduced to formal customs and walked down the path of corruption.

So both newly established and traditional Buddhist religions share the same mistaken view of our Buddha-nature: they think of enlightenment as something that can be attained with little effort. In other words, they seem to discount the original idea that we need effort to attain buddhahood and want to downplay the preconditions for attaining it by promising that anyone can achieve it effortlessly.

Consider this analogy: We, human beings can sail across the seas to reach foreign lands. We have the potential to sail the vast oceans of the Pacific or the Atlantic and reach the lands that lie beyond them. However, if this idea doesn't persuade people to make their own journey, and if we redefine the ocean voyage into something more manageable, we reach a point where we're saying that crossing the ocean is like jumping over a puddle—and anyone is capable of accomplishing this in a single leap. So the original spirit of the journey is completely lost.

What purpose was the journey originally meant to serve? Was the original aim of Buddhist training to help people jump puddles? Was that what spiritual development was for? Is that what enlightenment is all about?

For a small insect like a whirligig beetle that lives on the surfaces of water, crossing a puddle is a major achievement. But is there any sense of achievement that we human beings can gain in simply stepping over a rain puddle on a country road? Does this give us any joy? Does this give us any opportunity to gain spiritual training? The answer is that it doesn't help us accomplish any of these things.

Consider a man who is about to cross the Pacific Ocean in a yacht. He is bound to encounter great adversity on his voyage. The sun may beat down; there may be rain. He may run out of food and water. His muscles may ache, and he may suffer sunburns. But amid the severe hardships of his attempted ocean crossing, his soul is being strengthened. He is being refined. His inner thinking is deepened by his confrontation with the vastness of the ocean.

He goes through an experience that no one else has had, and he may try to tell others what a wonderful experience sailing the ocean can be. His story moves others to see that they too could cross an ocean and inspires them to embark on their own journey, first by practicing rowing or sailing their boats in the bay.

But what if, 2,600 years after his death, people have come to equate the feat of crossing an ocean with the act of crossing a puddle in a single stride? How would this man feel—a man who had sailed across the Pacific Ocean and returned to tell others of this wonderful experience? I am certain that he would want to explain in protest that he never said this endeavor would be as easy as jumping over a puddle.

2
Returning to the Original Teachings of the Buddha

If Shakyamuni were to see the condition that Buddhism is in now in some parts of our world, he would empathize with this man who made the ocean voyage. For forty-five years, Shakyamuni taught people to strengthen their minds and attain a higher state of mind. But his true teachings and the process of spiritual training he left behind are no longer taught. It's deeply regrettable to see that ideas of easy salvation that say, "You can find salvation just by doing such and such," have become so widespread in Buddhism.

As a consequence, even when religions with right teachings, such as Happy Science, appear—religions that aim to bring salvation to humanity and offer many splendid teachings for addressing the various stages of our soul growth—many people are unable to recognize the value of these teachings. This is why people come to us confused, unable to grasp my teachings, and asking just to be told to whom they should pray to gain salvation.

In other religions, people are instructed to do certain things, for instance, to pray to Amida Buddha, worship

Kannon (the goddess of mercy), or chant some sutras. Since they're used to being taught practices such as burning incense or putting their hands together in prayer and reciting the Lotus Sutra for their ancestors, newcomers to our organization often ask us, "Tell me, in a word, what do your teachings ask me to do?" And when they don't get a clear answer from us, they criticize us, saying, "Yours is a strange religion," "It's not a religion at all," "Your teachings are hard to grasp," and so on. But people who say these sorts of things misunderstand Shakyamuni's true intentions.

If we look at the teachings that Shakyamuni Buddha left behind, we see that he took into consideration the fact that we, as individuals, have different tendencies: he gave different teachings to cater to different kinds of people so that anyone could attain enlightenment. There are said to be eighty-four thousand sutras, an almost inexhaustible abundance. In terms of sheer quantity, Buddhism has hundreds or even thousands of times more teachings than Christianity, and the teachings are very deep and profound. All these different teachings arose solely from Shakyamuni's intention to bring each living person across to the shore of enlightenment. These teachings were later compiled by his disciples into what we now know as the sutras.

However, many people today are unable to understand what the mind is. Some imagine that our mind is a function of the nervous system, while others think our mind resides in the brain. Others think that our mind is a collection of chemical or electrical processes that respond to stimuli and that human beings are, after all, machines that function like computers. As a result of these misconceptions, people have come to see the Buddha's teachings about the mind and the spirit world as empty, abstract theories or even as fables and metaphors. This is perhaps a consequence of the materialism and excessive rationalism that began to prevail as a result of philosophical teachings that emerged after Kant. So we have to return to the Buddha's original teachings and study again with humility what they teach us.

3
Gaining a Thorough Understanding of the World of Our Mind

The world of the mind is indeed invisible. But just because we can't see it doesn't mean that the mind doesn't exist. Our inner world is our very essence as human beings, and it's wrongheaded to try to prove its existence with experiments that measure chemical reactions. The mind definitely exists and accepting this completely is the first step to our enlightenment.

The mind is invisible to our eyes and impossible to touch with our hands, but it exists in every human being. You possess a mind, as others also do. And if you observe deeply enough, you will see that it also exists in animals and plants, although their souls may not be as advanced as our own. Gaining this awareness of our mind's existence is your first step toward enlightenment. Without this awareness, we humans have no other choice but to live like machines.

The existence of our mind may seem like a difficult concept to understand, but ask yourself this: We human beings can experience happiness. How is this possible?

Children become happy when they eat something delicious or when parents or teachers praise them. But what allows them to become happy?

You, too, may feel happy when you eat something delicious. Do you think that this is because you are a machine being run by a nervous system that generates happy feelings when you receive input? Of course, some sort of chemical reaction may be involved in the process. But have you ever seen a machine experience happiness? Have you ever heard of a cog getting excited when it was oiled? Or a car that smiled at you when you filled it with fuel? I'm sure that you haven't. But unlike machines, we are able to experience happiness. Why is this possible?

We're able to experience happiness because we're capable of realizing through our consciousness when our wishes are answered and this gives rise to feelings of happiness in our mind. Without this ability, we'd be leading lives like machines. Even when a machine is given lubrication to help it work more smoothly it's not able to feel any joy. So the ability to feel is quite a wonderful thing—it means that a presiding entity exists within you that feels.

It is said in Buddhism that human beings have six sensory organs—the eyes, the ears, the nose, the tongue, the tactile body, and the mind—and six senses—sight, hearing, smell, taste, touch, and consciousness. Consciousness is the part of us that makes cognitive judgments made by our nervous system. For instance, you feel happy when you eat something delicious; this phenomenon is caused by the sense of taste. Your sense of taste transmits the feeling of deliciousness somewhere. But where does it transmit it to? Where does it transmit its feelings of pleasure, joy, and happiness? There must be another part of you that receives these sensations.

The fact that we experience these sensations means that there is a part of us making judgments about them. The same tongue can experience sweetness when licking something sweet, sourness when licking something sour, saltiness when having something salty, and acute pain when something burning hot touches our tongue. This means that there is some part of us that sends out these sensations and another part that receives them. In a word, it is our mind that receives them.

Let me give you another example. When parents or teachers praise a child, the child experiences happiness. This involves a higher level of perception. In this case, the sense of hearing is involved, which you could say is simply the vibration of the eardrum. But how does the vibrating of the eardrum make a child feel happy? Is it the way the eardrum vibrates that determines whether the child experiences happiness? Imagine, for instance, a robust male teacher who shouts out, "Hey! You got full marks! Congratulations!" and his voice is so loud that the windowpane almost shatters. In this situation, the eardrums feel such a strong vibration that they might cause physical pain. But despite the loud voice booming, "You got full marks on the exam," the child would feel not discomfort but, rather, happiness.

If, on the other hand, the teacher is a gentle female, who says in a soft voice, "Well, dear, you've done very well. You got full marks!" On hearing this the child would also feel happiness. In this situation, the type of vibration in the child's eardrums would be completely different from the situation with the male teacher. This time, the vibration would feel like a breeze. But no matter whether the sound is like a strong, gusty wind or a soft, gentle breeze, the child experiences pleasant feelings when being praised.

However, if you are being told off in a loud voice, you experience intimidation and fear. Similarly, if someone makes an offensive remark in a low voice, this can be upsetting; it may even reduce you to tears. This means that it is not simply the physical vibration that makes you feel happy. Although musical sounds may seem like a physical phenomenon, it is the consciousness deep within you that actually enjoys the music, after the vibrations have already passed through the eardrums and the brain. If we were just machines, we would not be able to notice the difference between the sound of someone hitting a bucket and playing the drums. But we have minds that receive information through the six senses and makes judgments about the pleasantness or unpleasantness of what we're sensing.

4
The Same Principle of the Mind Applies to Our Value Judgments

Through my spiritual abilities, I have found that it is not only we human beings living in physical bodies on earth who have perceptual senses. Spirits in the other world no longer have physical bodies, so they don't have the six sense organs of the body, but they still respond with the same feelings that they had when they were living in this world.

Spirits don't have physical ears, but they can still hear the voices of people on earth. They have no eardrums, but they can continue to listen to music. If their favorite song is being played, they can enjoy it even if they have become spirits. Conversely, they continue to dislike the music they previously disliked. So, as spirits, we retain the same ability to feel these sensations, even after we've left our physical bodies. We experience these feelings in the mind.

Of course, our intellect is also a function of our mind. In a purely worldly sense, some people are known to demonstrate high intelligence, while others demonstrate duller intelligence and they used to say that there are more folds in the brain of a bright person than those who are slower. But in reality, even if the physical body and brain have been lost, the thinking function continues to exist within the soul.

In Western medicine, a person suffering from anencephaly, the congenital absence of a brain, is sometimes treated as less than human. This idea is mistaken, because we don't think with our brains; the part of us that does the thinking lies beyond the brain organ, within the mind. The brain organ is more like a computer, a calculator, or a word processor if you will—a machine that processes information. If this machine breaks down, our physical body will have difficulty dealing with information, but our *soul* will still receive information accurately.

So the part of us that receives information about the various experiences of this world and makes judgments about whether they are good or bad, beautiful or ugly, and pleasant or unpleasant is our mind. What makes us human is our mind; otherwise we would be nothing more than objects moving haphazardly on earth. Because we have minds, we are human, and we have innate worth.

Strangely enough, the mind functions according to the same principles in different people, even though they were born to different parents. Our perceptions of good and bad, beautiful and ugly—these are fairly universal perceptions.

Although each person attaches different meanings to things and makes different judgments about them, everyone's perception of beauty when beholding something beautiful and of a sweet flavor when eating something sugary are similar. Two people living on opposite ends of the world still experience the same sense of sweetness when they eat something sweet. Generation after generation, for thousands or even tens of thousands of years, even though our families have lived in completely different places, we all perceive flavors of sweetness or spiciness, regardless of where we come from. We respond with laughter when we're happy and with tears when we're sad. Similar kinds of situations will instill anger. Although we may see small variations from person to person, we all react in the same way to the same conditions.

Why do we all share the same responses to these experiences? Because, regardless of the differences in our languages, the principles of the mind apply congruously to all people.

5
How Buddha-Nature Manifests

This is in fact related to how our Buddha-nature manifests in our mind. Our Buddha-nature is the common quality within us all that feels and experiences the different events of this world in similar ways. This is the beginning of Buddha-nature's manifestation. In a dark world, we all sense the darkness, and in a bright world we all sense the brightness. If you become happy, you feel joy. The fact that we all share similar ways of feeling these things is evidence that everyone possesses Buddha-nature.

Possessing Buddha-nature, the nature of enlightenment, means that every person's soul has the potential to make similar value judgments. If we were all by ourselves, we would feel and think in a certain way. We'd make judgments, saying to ourselves, "If it goes this way, I'll feel happy; if it goes another way, I'll feel unhappy." If we had perfect freedom to do everything in our own way, we would go in the direction that delighted ourselves and made ourselves happy.

In reality, though, we live on earth with many other people, as well as animals and plants, so we must consider whether our individual happiness also leads to the happiness of others. If we were alone, we'd have complete freedom, but we would miss out on the happiness to be found in relationships with others.

Suppose you are married and have a family. What makes you happy? Every morning, you go to the office, and after working hard from morning to night, sometimes getting told off by your boss, you come home tired. There may be times when you also need to fulfill social obligations to succeed at work. If you repeat this day in and day out, there may be times when you want to avoid going to work and would rather just stay home and sleep. This feeling might represent your personal happiness. But you also have a spouse and children to support. A financial basis is essential to your establishing a strong marriage and family. And to secure a financial foundation, you have to do work that gives value to society and that will earn you a living. Your salary is essential for taking care of the day-to-day living expenses and costs of raising children, so you have to go to work, even if it's unpleasant.

This judgment is totally separate from our natural emotions of like and dislike. For the sake of a higher purpose, you suppress your feelings of like and dislike and make your commute so you can be at work every day. Ordinarily, you wouldn't hesitate to follow your sense of like and dislike to avoid, for example, experiencing fatigue, feeling hot and sweaty on the bus, or having cramped and aching legs. But if these hardships are necessary for a higher happiness, such as the safety and future of your family, or your family's happiness at home, you endure them.

People who live alone can, indeed, enjoy more freedom. But when our goal is to share our happiness with others in the framework of relationships, we make the effort to limit a part of our freedom in favor of the good of the whole society. We try to create harmony with others to bring about the progress and development of the whole. For this reason, we put limits on our instincts, practice some level of self-sacrifice, and act in ways that create higher levels of happiness.

To put it simply, at a very primitive level, our Buddha-nature initially finds expression in basic emotions such as delight, anger, sorrow, and pleasure, and like and dislike. At the next stage, coexisting with others in communities, we inevitably find ourselves in situations that require us to restrain our basic feelings and preferences to create a higher order of happiness. In these situations, the ability to choose wisely is a higher-level manifestation of our Buddha-nature.

In making these choices, we often follow a basic rule that tells us that making certain choices and judgments in certain situations will lead us closer to happiness. For instance, hitting someone in a boxing match is different from hitting someone in an ordinary fight. Hitting a person in a fight makes both parties unhappy, but in a boxing match, hitting is regulated by specific rules. By participating in the sport of boxing, boxers develop their muscles and, whether they win or lose, find a higher level of happiness in making the effort to strive for a particular goal.

We human beings have created a number of invisible values. These invisible values arose out of certain principles that encouraged us to master our own free will so we can realize a higher purpose beyond ourselves: the happiness of all humanity. These principles were those that originated from our very Buddha-nature, or our inner nature of enlightenment.

6

Aspiring to Realize Buddha's Ideal

We exist, first and foremost, as individuals in this physical world. Since each individual originates from Buddha's Light, to attain happiness we each need to fully express our own particular qualities. On the other hand, we live not alone but hand in hand with others, so we must live for our common happiness. How do we balance these two kinds of happiness—the happiness of the individual and the happiness of the whole?

Throughout history, humans have created religions, philosophies and moral codes to answer this question. They all sought to offer teachings and principles that would enable large groups of people to live happily together. Philosophers used intellectual and rational approaches to develop their principles. Moralists developed principles that would serve as rules of everyday living. Religions drew on the perspective of God or Buddha to create their principles and also focused on cultivating a happiness that would be valid in both this world and the other. This is how religion came into being.

We and all living things in this world, including plants, are seeking our own happiness, but we also need to make use of our own lives to serve the happiness of others. If there is a conflict of interests in these two intentions, then we need to make an effort to bring them into harmony. This is Buddha's ideal. The part of us that affirms the value and wonder of Buddha's ideal is called Buddha-nature. Buddha-nature is the aspiration and willingness to respond to Buddha's ideal.

Those who have abandoned this way of thinking and live in quite an opposite way—those who shamelessly abuse or denounce Buddha's ideal—are considered to have "sold their souls to the devil." But that doesn't mean that they didn't originally have a Buddha-nature. They're going against their Buddha-nature simply because they're misguided or because a veil of delusion is covering their eyes and preventing them from seeing.

So Buddha-nature exists within every individual. It's the part of your mind that strives to practice Buddha's ideal. What is the ideal that Buddha wants us to realize? Buddha wishes for each of us to shine our brightest inner light as we strive to live harmoniously with the ideals of society and work to advance those ideals.

In this chapter, I have answered the question, "What is Buddha-nature?" in rather broad terms that relate to our everyday lives. I hope this chapter will serve as a useful guide on your journey to enlightenment.

THREE

THE ESSENCE OF ZEN MEDITATION

1

The Purpose of Zen Meditation

This chapter will explore the meaning of *zenjo*, or Zen meditation, in depth. On hearing the words "Zen meditation," perhaps you may think of sitting in a cross-legged posture or practicing yoga. This is probably a natural reaction, because it is true that these methods are used in Zen meditation. But regrettably, many people seem to misunderstand Zen meditation, thinking that it's merely the physical training of sitting in a particular posture.

Many people who practice Zen meditation do not seem to have ever considered its purpose very deeply; instead, they seem conscious only of its form or style. But I believe that this topic deserves further exploration. So here, let us think once again about the true purpose of Zen meditation.

The Japanese Zen master Dogen (1200–1253 CE) introduced a style of meditation called "Shikantaza," which means "simply sitting silently without a purpose." Dogen was the founder of one of the major schools of Zen, and this method of meditation has long been accepted as an important part of Zen training. In yoga, too, which originated in India and spread to China, there are many styles of meditation, but it appears that some of these are directed only at maintaining health or are practiced as physical disciplines. Although yoga is certainly a method of meditation that has been handed down through the ages, I have the impression that those who practice it are seeking the essence of Zen meditation only from a three-dimensional, physical perspective.

Where did Zen meditation originate? Zen meditation itself is not the invention of Gautama Siddhartha, also known as Shakyamuni Buddha. In India, it was a traditional practice long before the time of Shakyamuni. In religions other than Buddhism, too, people practice a method of developing mental concentration that resembles Zen meditation. So in this sense, meditation practice has always been associated with religion.

So for what purpose should we practice Zen meditation? Simply put, our purpose is to communicate with the heavenly world or the world of high spirits. Those who do not understand this may meditate for health or may simply think that it's good to spend time just sitting without thinking about anything and without a purpose. This may indeed be one style of spiritual discipline that people can practice. But this is not the purpose of meditation. If meditation were only a matter of sitting still, trees and stones could do it much better than we can. If the whole purpose of our spiritual training in life were to become immovable like a mountain, then we might as well have been born trees or stones. But human beings are not trees or stones. We have hearts and minds, and that is the essence of being human.

The three-dimensional world where we lead our daily lives is filled with coarse thought vibrations, and many of these worldly thoughts are quite negative. In daily life, your mind may become disturbed, for example, when you hear shocking news or after arguing with someone. When you hear sad news, your mind may waver. You may lose yourself when you get drunk and sing in a bar. Sometimes, you must isolate yourself from all these daily activities, cut yourself off from the vibrations of the third dimension, and ask what your true self is. This act of rediscovering your authentic self is the true essence of Zen meditation.

2
Refining the Vibrations of the Mind

Although the basic posture of Zen meditation is sitting cross-legged, you don't necessarily have to stick to this posture. The first step is to distance yourself from daily life, and to do this, you need to find a place where you won't be disturbed by worldly vibrations. Avoid noisy places and rooms where the telephone might ring or where people often go in and out. Choose a quiet place where you won't be interrupted for some time, and create a calm environment so you can concentrate on your dialogue with yourself.

After shutting out the outside world, gradually tune your mind in to a calmer and calmer wavelength. Human beings constantly emit certain mental vibrations, but when we quiet them down, our thought vibrations become separated from various coarse vibrations of the three-dimensional world. Once you enter this calm state and detach yourself from your everyday life in the physical world, your mind will no longer waver, and disturbing thoughts about various people and everyday matters will gradually recede. You'll begin to feel as relaxed as if you were somewhere in a village deep in the mountains or lying on a beach all day long. This is the first stage of Zen meditation.

To escape the vibrations of the third dimension and discover your true self, it's first necessary to relax your physical body. Choose the posture that's most comfortable for you. You don't have to keep to the traditional Indian posture of sitting cross-legged. That posture is fine for people who are accustomed to it, but for many modern people, sitting that way will distract their minds because they will be constantly conscious of their posture. Remember that the first thing to do is calm your mind and relax your body.

When your body is relaxed, gradually regulate your breathing: inhale and exhale deeply from the abdomen. Repeat this deep breathing slowly and rhythmically. Oxygen will circulate throughout your body, and that will slowly and gradually settle down your heart. Your brain waves will become more subtle and calm, freeing your mind from the concerns of everyday life.

Regulating your breathing has another good effect on the physical body. As oxygen-rich blood circulates through the body, it replaces any fatigued blood congested in the brain. When you come under negative spiritual influences, you're usually affected in the parts of the body where blood has become congested or where fatigue has accumulated; for instance, at the back of the head, the neck, the shoulders, and the lower back. Parts that become stiff are in fact points where stray spirits can attach themselves. These spirits sense and respond to the wavelengths of inharmonious vibrations from the physical body, and when the two correspond with one another, possession can often occur.

Those who are constantly affected by negative spiritual influences or easily fall under the control of stray spirits must be especially mindful of this. Those who feel exhausted when they go out or who feel very heavy and tired in crowded places are vulnerable to possession. So first of all, it's very important to regulate and calm the rhythms of the physical body. Breathe in and take in fresh oxygen. Visualize the blood circulating throughout your entire body, from your head to your neck, your shoulders, and your back. This will gradually eliminate inharmonious vibrations throughout your body.

To remove less serious possession, it's best to begin by regulating the physical body this way. When you feel exhausted, it usually means that blood is congested in some part of your body. Light aerobic exercise will help improve the blood's circulation and allow you to receive more Light. After exercising, gradually relax your body and regulate your breathing. As you let go of the worldly vibrations associated with concerns of the third dimension, your mind will settle into a calmer wavelength, and as you begin to feel calmer, feelings of joy and happiness should well up from within you. This feeling of happiness is proof that you are regaining your original self, though you may still only sense this rather vaguely. Refining the vibrations of the mind is essential to Zen meditation, because otherwise it's extremely difficult to communicate with the Spirit World.

3
Surface Consciousness and the Subconscious

If you become absorbed in mental concentration without first calming the vibrations of your mind, you may become more vulnerable to possession and may even be severely affected by negative spiritual influences. To avoid this, always keep your mind serene before entering a meditative state. If you practice concentration while your mind is filled with anger, complaints, or discontent, malicious spirits and demons can easily possess you.

Because we live in the three-dimensional world and are usually concerned only with physical matters, our minds can easily assimilate to the wavelengths of the third dimension. This has both positive and negative effects. The advantage is that exclusively tuning in to the wavelengths of the physical world can make it difficult for stray spirits to possess us, because it's often hard for them to keep up with people who work busily every day. The disadvantage of a busy life, though, is that it makes it extremely difficult for divine spirits to send us inspiration. When we enter a meditative state, we're subject to both positive and negative spiritual influences.

You may have come across the terms "surface consciousness" and "subconscious." Before we can contact the Spirit World, the door to our subconscious needs to be open, and to open it, we have to gradually quiet our surface consciousness.

Surface consciousness come to the fore when the brain is working to the full and functioning constantly; for instance, when we engage in debate, do calculations and paperwork, or talk on the phone at the office. When we relax, on the other hand, the brain's mental activity calms down, and our consciousness sinks below the surface. And in turn, the subconscious, which is usually hidden deep within, starts to surface. The inner world then emerges—a world made purely of the images we hold in our mind, which often resembles our experiences in dreams.

When the door to the subconscious opens, we face the possibility of contacting both heaven and hell. Those who always live in a good-hearted way, who try to have good thoughts and do good deeds, can easily start contacting high-level spirits, such as their guardian and guiding spirits, as soon as they quiet their surface consciousness. But those who have few good thoughts and hardly ever endeavor to do good deeds are very likely to come under negative spiritual influences.

The method of Zen meditation that I'm describing here is strongly related to your everyday thoughts and actions, or what you're thinking and doing at the present moment. Ordinarily, people don't even think about correcting their state of mind or exploring Right Mind. Although some may have studied the concept of right and wrong in philosophy classes at one time, they've probably never thought deeply about it in the course of their daily lives. Only those with a religious disposition are likely to constantly check on their thoughts to see whether they're right or wrong. Usually, people don't make a habit of checking what's in their mind, nor are most people aware of whether the thought they just had was wrong or right. Most people are not in the habit of examining each of their actions and saying to themselves, "I did the right thing" or "I did something wrong."

But as you study the Truth at Happy Science, you'll become more spiritual and contemplative and will gain the ability to examine your thoughts one by one. You'll be able to say, "This is a good thought," "This is a bad thought," or "I've just had a wrong thought." You can do the same thing with your actions. If you can develop this habit, you'll be very unlikely to be affected by negative spiritual influences, even when you're in a state of mental concentration.

4
Removing the Rust from Your Mind: Self-Reflection

If you're not in the habit of checking your thoughts and deeds but would like to practice Zen meditation in your spare time, begin by shutting yourself off from worldly vibrations and calming the waves of your mind. When you feel that the door to your subconscious is about to open, polish your mind by removing any "rust" from your mind. When you have "bumps" in your mind, stray spirits can use them as hooks to tie a rope to and use that rope to pull themselves up into your mind. So before fully engaging yourself in interaction with your subconscious, you need to correct your state of mind by examining your thoughts and deeds one by one.

What should you examine first? Usually, it is most important to reflect on how your day went today. Ask yourself: What was your day like? What kinds of thoughts passed through your mind from the time you awoke? Were those thoughts right? Did you have any malicious thoughts toward others? Did you have any negative thoughts? Did you do anything wrong? In this way, you can reflect on your thoughts and actions for the day.

After you have examined your mind and found any wrong thoughts or actions, resolve not to repeat them. If you had wrong thoughts toward someone, repent and correct your thoughts. If you've done something wrong, make up your mind never to repeat the same mistake. When you've finished cleaning your mind for that day, extend your range further, and recall what happened over the past week. Thoroughly examine your thoughts and actions over the course of the week, checking whether they were right or wrong in the light of the Truth taught at Happy Science.

When you've done this, you can go back further and examine the past month. Review your thoughts and actions during the last month. Did you have any negative thoughts? Did you do anything wrong? Did you improve yourself in accordance with the Truth? Have you been making sufficient effort? Have you been fulfilling your mission as a disciple of Buddha? Have you accomplished what you were supposed to? How much progress have you made, compared with a month ago? If you haven't made any progress, you've been wasting the life that Buddha has given you. Are you thankful? Do you feel grateful that you are given life? Do you give thanks to Buddha and to all creation on this earth? Are you grateful to others for their help? Try reflecting back on your previous month in this manner.

Next, reflect on the past year. What were you doing around the same time a year ago? What have you thought about and done since then? Have you made any progress over the course of the year? Have you succeeded at solving your problems or improving your character? Are your character and your problems getting better or worse? You can reflect on the past year in this way. Through this process, you can purify both your body and your mind to a large degree.

If you have plenty of time, reflect on everything that has happened since you were born, dividing your life into several periods. For example, ask yourself what kind of child you were from birth to three years old. Project your life onto the screen of your mind as if you were seeing it on a movie screen. You'll see your parents, brothers and sisters, grandparents, neighbors, and all those who were around you. How do you appear in each scene? Then reflect further, up to the time you entered primary school. Reflect on yourself during your primary school days. What about junior school and high school? And after that? Reflect on each period, one at a time, recollecting the important turning points in your life, up until now. By this time, it's very likely that tears will be welling up in your eyes in spite of yourself. As these tears stream down your cheeks, they wash away the impurities of your mind.

5

From Self-Reflection to Meditation:
Reflective Meditation

As you reflect on your past, you'll quite naturally experience feelings of repentance and regret that bring tears, even though you were never told or taught to feel this way. These tears are the very evidence that you have Buddha-nature within you.

Some people may seem so wicked that it's as if they were born rogues or villains. But even these people cry tears of repentance when they reflect on their past thoughts and actions and realize how foolish they've been. The fact that we all have the ability to reflect on ourselves and become aware of our own foolishness is proof that every single one of us has Buddha-nature. Although there might be differences in the depth of our reflection or in the way we live, deep in our hearts we all know what standards to use to judge whether we are right or wrong. This is why we shed tears when we realize our own errors during self-reflection. Our remorse is not a function of the brain, nor a function of the eyes; it is a strong emotion that wells up from the soul. It's a heartfelt emotion that we feel when we know our true self.

So relax, attune your mind and body, enter into a reflective mode, and examine your past. By the time you shed tears, your heart has begun to be purified and become transparent. Needless to say, it's not enough to do this just once; you have to repeat this self-reflection over and over from time to time. It's difficult to reflect on the past all at once, especially if you've already lived a long time; you'll need to divide your life into several periods and recall them in order. I suggest that you choose a time and place to reflect deeply on your past every now and then, since you may forget the things that you've reflected on after a year or so.

By reflecting on yourself, you can gradually calm your mind and relax your spirit until you reach a state of deep concentration. This is what we call "reflective meditation." This is the method Shakyamuni Buddha always used to enter a meditative state. If you are a religious practitioner, you may find it quite easy to concentrate your mind, but you may face an increasing risk of possession by evil spirits if you concentrate your mind without practicing reflective meditation first. To avoid this danger, you need to practice self-reflection before going deep into the recesses of your mind. Self-reflection allows you to practice fruitful concentration with very little risk.

As you reflect on yourself and enter a meditative state, your mind will become more distinctly separate from this three-dimensional world, and gradually tap into the treasure house of the subconscious. Your real self is now stepping into "the real world," the world you originally came from. This is the world of meditation.

6

The Source of Spiritual Energy: The Essence of Zen Meditation

As you enter the state of meditation, your mind leaves this three-dimensional world and becomes immersed in other dimensions—the fourth dimension and beyond. You can tell which world your soul originally came from by observing which world your true self visits and which spirits your true self communicates with during meditation.

If you were to die while in a state of meditation, your soul would go to a place in the other world that corresponds exactly to the state of mind you had attained at that time. Your destination after your death will be determined by how refined your mind is at the time. If your state of mind corresponds to a kind of hell, you will go to hell, and if it corresponds to heaven, you will return to the level in the heavenly world that matches your state of mind.

When we die, we return to the world that more or less corresponds to the level of thoughts that we habitually have. But strangely enough, our minds each have a certain capacity that limits the level of our thoughts, so even if we try to think the very highest thoughts, we can only go as high as our mind is capable of.

It's quite possible for most people to return to heaven, but will you become a bodhisattva? How high a level of heaven will you ascend to? The answers to these questions have a lot to do with how much progress you make in expanding your mind's capacity through constant and diligent efforts as you go through your life.

However, you won't be able to reach the highest level of spiritual awareness all at once just from your spiritual training in this lifetime alone. The soul training you went through in your past lives and the spiritual capacity you've acquired through countless other incarnations also help determine your destination in the other world.

It is the overall capacity of the soul that determines the extent to which the treasure house of the subconscious can be opened. But as I've repeatedly said, our spiritual training in this lifetime will help us get rid of our mental rust and impurities and refine our minds, and this helps each of us communicate with our own guardian spirit. So by making an effort in our present life, all of us can at least reach the stage of Arhat, the state of mind corresponding to the upper realms of the sixth dimension.*

If you make a habit of cleaning and concentrating your mind, you'll naturally be able to communicate with

* See chapter 4 of *The Laws of the Sun* (New York: IRH Press, 2018) and chapter 6 of *The Essence of Buddha* (New York: IRH Press, 2016).

your guardian spirit and your other soul siblings, all of whom reside in the world of your subconscious.* This experience will give you a feeling of bliss that is beyond words. You will feel that they are always watching over you with an affectionate gaze and supporting you in your everyday life. You'll feel thankful and warm inside, and that will naturally make you want to be good to everyone around you.

Zen meditation doesn't exist just for its own sake. Practicing Zen meditation gives you a chance to communicate with the world from which you originate and to glimpse images of the ideal world. You'll also receive Light from the other world through your brother or sister souls or more advanced guiding spirits. You can then transform this Light into a source of vitality and energy for your everyday life. This is the essence of Zen meditation.

Through Zen meditation, you can regularly correct the orbit of your life and acquire a renewed zest for living, which you can use as a source of spiritual energy to spread goodness in this world. For these reasons, Zen meditation is tremendously important. I hope that you will once again return to the starting point and think deeply about refining your mind, using this chapter as your reference.

---

* The soul is made up of six individual energies called "soul siblings." These soul siblings take turns being born on Earth. While we are living in the material world, one member of our soul sibling group acts as a guardian spirit. For more information, see chapter 2 of *The Laws of the Sun*.

FOUR

TRANSCENDENTAL WISDOM AND FORGIVING LOVE

1
What Is Transcendental Wisdom?

To understand what it means to achieve enlightenment in Buddhism, we need to understand the term *transcendental wisdom** (*panna* in Pali or *prajna* in Sanskrit). In this chapter, I offer an in-depth discussion about cultivating transcendental wisdom, including how it relates to the different developmental stages of love, which we often look at in contrast with the various stages in enlightenment.

Gaining transcendental wisdom is generally considered synonymous with attaining enlightmenment. I would like to explain why this has been the case.

Acquiring transcendental wisdom requires that we practice the correct attitude toward our daily spiritual development. Simply put, we need to continuously and carefully practice the three essentials of learning: keeping the precepts, meditating, and accumulating wisdom.

As you continuously control your daily thoughts and deeds according to the precepts, practice meditation, and

---

* I have offered a detailed explanation of this topic in *The Silent Buddha*. The original Japanese title of this book is *Chinmoku No Buddha* (Tokyo: IRH Press, 1993). This title is currently unavailable in English.

accumulate wisdom, you will eventually experience the state of liberation. This state of liberation allows you to attain the state of mind known as nirvana (*nibbana* in Pali). And transcendental wisdom is the inexplicably profound, crystal-clear wisdom that you gain in this state of nirvana.

Throughout the ages, Buddhist seekers of Truth have sought after this profound wisdom. They've constantly asked, "What is the true meaning of transcendental wisdom?" and "What are its results?" Since ancient times, these questions have been the common subjects of inquiry for Buddhist seekers.

So what does happen when we attain transcendental wisdom? The simple answer is that you will gain deep insight into your own being, the being of others, and the whole world. In other words, while you're still living in this three-dimensional world, you'll be able to clearly understand what kind of world you have been put in to serve what kind of purpose and with what kinds of relationships. To put it another way, transcendental wisdom helps us achieve the profound enlightenment that we aren't just living our lives proactively; instead, we're being given this life.

In contrast to this is intellectual perception (*vinnanna* in Pali and *vijnana* in Sanskrit) which is our inner sense that is consciously making proactive, dynamic, and positive choices for ourselves as we go through life. It's different with transcendental wisdom. Someone who has attained transcendental wisdom achieves a deep sense of being given life. Although an active and positive attitude toward life is also amply commendable, transcendental wisdom is a higher state of wisdom in which you realize that you and others are being given life and that this world exists to foster the lives of all of us.

Intellectual perception and transcendental wisdom differ because the intellect enables us to observe and analyze other people and the events that occur in society but doesn't let us observe our inner selves. Just as an index finger can point at others but not at itself and a sword can cut other things but not itself, the intellect allows us to understand others and the things of this world analytically, from the fixed standpoint of our ego, but not our inner selves.

In contrast, transcendental wisdom allows us to detach from the ego and see ourselves, others, and the things of this world vividly, as they truly are. We grow keenly aware that we are being enabled to live. We understand that the things in this world—whether they bring joy or sadness, suffering or anxiety—all exist to nurture our life. We see that everything in this world exists as material for learning and that this world is a valuable place of learning. Transcendental wisdom means knowing why this world exists, why you are living here and now, how you came to be born, and how you will come to leave this world.

When you develop your intellect, you gain the kind of wisdom that helps you make better choices in this world, improve yourself, and become exceptional—but it's a narrower perspective. Although this type of wisdom is very important for character building and self-improvement, it offers us only a limited range of understanding.

As we come to acquire transcendental wisdom, we realize that we have lived for an eternal time, reincarnating again and again in this vast universe of which the spirit world is a part, repeating the cycle of birth, life, death, and the afterlife. We understand that through these countless incarnations, we have come to know our own essence and the essence of the lives of others. We realize that we and everyone else are all here together to develop and refine our souls, like students living in the same era. And we start to see that although there are sad and painful experiences in this world, they are insubstantial. They are experiments in this material world, which is a training ground to refine our souls.

In the stage of transcendental wisdom, we understand that all beings are transient and essentially without ego. All things, including the physical body and the phenomena of this world, are transient. Everything changes and transforms constantly. Although things seem to exist around us, all of creation is really egoless. These things do not truly exist but are simply made to appear for a limited time by the will of the great universe to provide us with learning opportunities for our souls.

2
Intellectual Perception and Nurturing Love

Happy Science teaches that love consists of different developmental stages*. At the lowest stage is a type of love that takes from others and leads in the wrong direction. After this comes the stage of instinctive love. Instinctive love is followed by fundamental love, a typical type of giving love. Above fundamental love is nurturing love, a highly advanced form of giving love. And finally, there is forgiving love, a love practiced by those who have experienced a deep spiritual awakening.

As I explained above, intellectual perception is very much like awareness but is mainly focused on using the six physical senses—sight, hearing, smell, taste, touch, and consciousness—to make rational or sensory judgments. The intellect may also give rise to a higher level of spiritual perception, but it's still only a limited aspect of the soul—it generally only rises to the sixth-dimensional level of perception. Intellect alone cannot raise your awareness beyond this level. To go to the world of the seventh

---

* See chapter 3 of *The Laws of the Sun*.

dimension or higher, you must become aware of your spiritual essence and gain a deep sense of the spirit world.

Intellectual perception can have some spiritual aspects, but it's essentially a mental faculty that can only be developed within this three-dimensional world where we progress by clearly distinguishing between the self and others and competing with one another.

In this sense, intellectual perception is closely related to the development of love up to the stage of nurturing love, because the ability to distinguish between good and evil is a vital foundation for practicing nurturing love. You have to be able to distinguish between good and evil or superior and inferior to understand how you need to develop yourself.

If everyone stopped developing in kindergarten, could society continue to progress? Just as kindergarten children are not yet developed enough to understand good and evil, you need to develop yourself so you can tell the difference between good and evil. As you go through this process of establishing your self-growth, you will also witness the self-growth achieved by others.

So we go through life distinguishing ourselves from others, and develop rules based on the relationships we see arising between people. We use these rules to distinguish right from wrong: we learn that following the rules is good and breaking them is bad. So rules are basically what most people accept as a good way to live, and they serve as worldly criteria for distinguishing between good and evil.

To grow spiritually, it's very important to try to observe the rules of this world. In fact, we can't refine our souls if we don't try to follow the rules. As we establish our sense of self, it's extremely important for our spiritual training that we study our relationships with others and learn how we should live in relation to other people. As you can see, understanding good and evil and learning the rules for distinguishing between them is a major part of our spiritual training in this world.

3
Looking into the Origins of Good and Evil

When you can see beyond intellectual perception and see things from the higher standpoint of transcendental wisdom, you begin to clearly see how the rules of this world originated and why we created them. To reach this perspective, you need to look at why these rules became necessary.

Let's look at an example: our awareness of the differences between men and women. Some people may simply recognize that men and women are different. Others may take this a step further and conclude that it is not good to discriminate between genders and that we all should be treated as equals. As a result of trying to determine how men and women can best coexist in this three-dimensional world, we developed many rules. But it's hard to develop such rules by focusing solely on the values of this world.

To understand why both men and women exist, we need to think deeply about how the divine created the world. When our understanding deepens enough that we can see the differences in the souls of our two genders rather than differences in our physical appearances, we gain fresh insight into how we develop our souls in this world, and this knowledge can be the basis to a rule.

Another example to use in contemplating the origin of rules is criminal law, where we find rules such as "do not kill other human beings" and "do not steal." You may understand these rules subjectively to mean that you should not do anything you would not like others to do to you. However, a more profound perspective will help you see that these acts are wrong because they go against the ideal of Buddha when He created humankind.

When people argue about saving or putting an end to someone's physical life, the conclusion they generally reach is that preserving life is good and destroying life is evil. It's true that our lives in this world are limited and everyone dies eventually, but when we truly understand that Buddha has entrusted each of us with His ideal of respecting ourselves and others and creating utopia on earth, then our perspective becomes even more profound.

This perspective can change our views on crime. Good and evil do exist in this three-dimensional world. They were first defined by philosophy and ethics, and in modern society, laws often reflect and enforce our sense of good and bad. For actions that are not covered by specific laws, common sense is used as a standard for determining whether actions are good or bad, and people are usually offended by what is bad and will take action against it.

However, when we develop a deeper perspective based on transcendental wisdom, we come to understand the qualities of our Buddha-nature—the memory lying deep within our souls—and use this knowledge to determine whether or not particular thoughts and actions help the Buddha-nature within us all shine through.

Before reaching this state of transcendental wisdom, we of course need to be able to recognize good and evil from a worldly perspective. But we also need to develop the ability to see through to the origin of good and evil. When we reach this level, we clearly understand the nature of the evil that exists in this world. We come to see that evil does not really exist in and of itself but arises when people come into conflict with one another, because we all wish to live and develop in our own way.

Evil arises in relation to people, times, and places. In other words, evil arises in the relationships between people, when proper place and timing has been disregarded, and when there has been an error of judgment about our position in relation to others. Our behaviors can give rise to evil when we direct them toward the wrong person. There are things you should not do to other people, even if it is not a problem when you do those things to your spouse. There are things you are encouraged to do with your own children but not with the children of others. Likewise, there are things you are allowed to do with business associates but not with others. The situation changes according to the people you're interacting with.

Similarly, the timing of your actions also makes a difference. There are things that you should only do early in the morning, only in the middle of the day, and only in the evening. For instance, if you're in the habit of indulging in sleep during the day and getting up in the middle of the night, you may have difficulty adapting yourself to society. There are also actions that minors are considered too young for. Those who are underage are prohibited from drinking and smoking, because these actions are harmful to them both physically and mentally.

Errors can also arise from wrong judgments regarding location. While it's acceptable for children to be mischievous at kindergarten, playing a trick on someone in an office would create confusion, so it would most likely be considered wrong. Screaming in a crowded train would also be considered inappropriate. So whether a person's actions are good or bad also depends on where they take place. As you can see, the relationship between people, time, and place is an important determining factor for distinguishing between good and evil.

4

Seeing the World from the Perspective of Your Guardian Spirit

As I have explained, good and evil manifest in relation to several factors: people, times, and places. An action is considered good if it fosters harmony among everyone, but it's considered evil if it gives rise to discord. So when you encounter disharmony, you should delve into it to find its root cause—that is until you can identify the specific thoughts and actions that gave rise to the disharmony.

To take this a step further, you should consider how people have developed their own particular way of thinking. Did they acquire incorrect knowledge? Did their home background lead them to think in a particular way? Are their decisions the result of previous lives' karma or a tendency in their thinking? In this way, examine the patterns in each person's thoughts and actions. What caused this particular person to do this? What will the result be of what the person is doing now? If this person continues to live without changing his or her ways, what might happen? As you continue to look at how different people behave, as if you were looking at them from the perspective of your guardian spirit above, you will see things from a perspective of transcendental wisdom.

Transcendental wisdom develops your ability to see yourself and others, your environment, your family, and your company or school as your guardian spirit sees them. You can look at everything from the perspective of your guardian spirit: each day of your life, your whole life, your relationships with friends and family, and your relationships with society and with the times you're living in. Acquiring this perspective is a very important aspect of your spiritual development and one that leads you toward transcendental wisdom.

In the course of your life, you may have a major quarrel with someone and carry your hatred toward that person in your heart for many years. You may also experience many types of failure or face accidents. You may fall ill or suffer an injury. In fact, it's impossible to avoid these sorts of undesirable events. Whenever things like this happen, I would like you to try to imagine how these events look to your guardian spirit. If you make a habit of reviewing each of your experiences this way, you'll begin to understand them more deeply, rather than seeing them as simply good or bad or as things you like or dislike.

Your guardian spirit knows your life plan and what you intended to accomplish in this lifetime. If you always try to look at yourself from this perspective, you'll gradually come to understand how your life appears to your guardian spirit's eyes. Even if you've taken a wrong turn at some point in the course of your life, you'll be able to find clues to what you can do to reshape your life from this point on.

Let's look at a few examples. Some of you may have complaints about your parents, but just imagine what would have happened to you if both of your parents had died immediately after your birth and you had been adopted or sent to an orphanage. Another example is a husband who always complains about his wife and blames her for his constant unhappiness. But imagine if he had never had the chance to marry anyone? Others feel dissatisfied with their educational background, complain that their alma mater was not their first choice, and see this as the cause of their unhappiness. But what if they had not been admitted to any university and had no opportunity to even get a degree? Still others complain about an illness, but what sort of life would they have had if they had been born disabled?

As you can see in these examples, when you examine your present life from a completely different angle, forgetting the past and starting with a clean slate, you can see your various problems anew. As if you're rewinding a tape and playing it over and over again, take a fresh look at your likes and dislikes, what you consider good and bad, and your relationships with the people around you. When you look at things from this level, you've come to reach a state of transcendental wisdom.

Then, you'll be able to stand back and see yourself with detachment. At present, you may grumble, "I don't like him, and maybe he doesn't like me either," "I'm not on good terms with my friend," "My colleague and I are angry with each other," "My wife and I are fed up with each other," "My children and I do not really love each other," and so on. But you can still stop, think, and calmly contemplate what would have happened if you had never had these relationships, if you had had a completely different life. This should lead you to consider the possibility of a completely different understanding of good and evil and help you realize that you might also have brought about unpleasant experiences for others.

5
Transcendental Wisdom and Forgiving Love

Being in a state of transcendental wisdom is very much like practicing forgiving love. In this stage of love, you deeply understand the pain and sorrow that people face while living in this world.

> Because we go through soul-training
> in a physical body,
> We all make so many mistakes as we go through life.
> The course of our lives are laden with mistakes
> of various kinds
> As we blindly feel our way forward through life.
> This is the very nature of our lives.
> In this life, we cannot but fumble our way
> through our journey,
> So we all inevitably make lots of mistakes.
> But let us understand our starting point:
> All of us are blindly feeling our way through
> the darkness of this world.
> Let's encourage one another.
> Let's look less at the evil in others

And think less of the good we do for others.
Let us, instead, live together in harmony,
Without looking to lock horns,
But live together as friends who are sharing an era.

This view of life illustrates a religious viewpoint that is characterized by forgiving love, and the state of transcendental wisdom is very close to this viewpoint. Both forgiving love and transcendental wisdom can be achieved only through a deep understanding of the origins of the universe, Buddha's will, the mission of human beings, the system of reincarnation, and the impermanence and egolessness of all beings.

6

A Religious Perspective and Spiritual Training

I have looked at transcendental wisdom and forgiving love from several angles, and before I conclude, I would like to mention some important points that need to be kept in mind. A person who has attained a religious perspective is able to take the view that the self and others are not separate, but one, and that good and evil are two sides of the same coin. But we can only reach this understanding after we've gained a profound insight into the deeper meaning of the self and others and the difference between good and evil as a result of making tireless efforts toward spiritual development.

Understanding that good and evil are two sides of the same coin is not the same as being unable to distinguish between them. If you see someone who is unable to tell good and evil apart, then you must teach them how. This is an extremely important lesson to give, because you can transcend good and evil only after you have learned to distinguish between them. We must understand the distinction between good and evil before we can begin to transcend this distinction. And to understand the difference between good and evil, you have to make a thorough study of what constitutes good and what constitutes evil.

For this reason, transcendental wisdom does not result in a simple, good-natured attitude that sees everything as good, nor does it give rise to confusion about good and evil. It does not offer any excuses for laziness in our spiritual training. Transcendental wisdom embodies a great enlightenment in which you cultivate an all-embracing perspective, an egoless mindset, and a heart that constantly wishes to draw closer to the void (*sunyata* in Sanskrit).

If you misunderstand this, if everything becomes confused and you then conclude that there is no such thing as good or evil or that there is no difference between good religions and misguided ones, it means that you are headed in a wrong direction and could end up falling off a steep cliff while under the illusion that you are on the right path and headed in the direction of progress and evolution. Remember that transcendental wisdom can only be attained as the result of constant effort to refine your soul. Watch out so that you can avoid the pitfall of conceit.

FIVE

THE BENEFITS OF AN EGOLESS PERSPECTIVE

1
The True Meaning of Egolessness

Time and again, I've given lectures on the topic of egolessness, and some of you may wonder why I'm discussing such an old-fashioned idea at this time or why I repeatedly speak about such an abstract teaching.* Or perhaps you want to know more than just that such a teaching exists—perhaps you also want to know why developing an egoless perspective is so important. To answer these questions, I would like to talk about the philosophical aspect of this teaching and explain the purpose it serves and the benefits of practicing it.

This topic may seem unusual for a book on Buddhist teachings. It's normal for pharmacists to explain the health benefits of their products, but Buddhists often hesitate to explain the practical advantages of following Buddha's teachings. Of course, there are some Buddhist groups that promise worldly benefits, but few, if any, have gone on to explain traditional Buddhist concepts such

* I have covered this topic in *The Challenge of Enlightenment* and *The Silent Buddha*. The original Japanese title of the latter book is *Chinmoku No Buddha*, and it is currently unavailable in English.

as egolessness from a practical perspective. With this in mind, let me take a pragmatic approach and shed light on why we should practice egolessness and the outcomes we can hope to gain from it.

To put it simply, egolessness teaches us to think that our ego, or who we think we are, doesn't truly exist. Some of you might argue, "You said that the ego doesn't exist, but look, here I am. If I were to hit the person in front of me and tell him that he isn't feeling any pain because his ego doesn't really exist, he'd still feel the pain," and you may conclude that what I've said is false. Others interpret egolessness to mean that everything perishes when we die, while others would say that the feeling of being alive in the present proves that we exist. Materialists might respond that because the human body's atoms and molecules ultimately decompose into carbon dioxide and water, we human beings have no real existence. And some also believe that there's no such thing as the human mind—that the idea of the mind is an abstraction of these organs' biological functions. But all these arguments are based on a misunderstanding.

Many complex philosophies have debated whether the ego really exists. But to begin this chapter's discussion, I would like you at least to understand this: Shakyamuni Buddha's teaching of egolessness was not a denial of our human existence.

Shakyamuni Buddha taught about the importance of spiritual training and never said things like, "You don't exist" or "I don't exist." If we didn't exist, there would be no need for us to practice discipline, effort, and perseverance. If he had said things like that, he would have been contradicting his dying words, "Everything is transient, so don't become attached to anything. Don't fall into languidness, but constantly strive to refine your soul." Denying our existence is like saying, "When you die, everything will disappear; nothing will remain of you." If that were true, Shakyamuni's dying words to his disciples about the importance of diligent discipline and self-refinement would have been groundless.

2
The Torch Within and the Torch of Dharma

As Shakyamuni passed away, he said:

"How very similar I am to the moon that disappears behind the clouds but continues to shine brightly beyond them. Just like the full moon that vanishes from time to time but reappears perfectly round when a gust of wind clears away the clouds, my life will seem to disappear from you, but only for a time.

"I will not completely disappear, nor will I be gone forever. Like the moon, I'll continue shining on as brightly as ever.

"I'll go into hiding for some time, and this holds a purpose: if I were to light this world constantly, you wouldn't light your own torch and illuminate your own path. This is my reason for disappearing from you, my disciples. So engrave in your heart that my death does not mean I've perished forever nor that I've ceased to exist."

He continued, "After I die, live your lives according to what I've asked of you in my teachings: let the torch within you and the torch of dharma remain lit." To light the torch within means to illuminate yourself through your own efforts and to depend upon yourself. Shakyamuni Buddha explained this inner torch in this way: In India, the rain sometimes falls violently and makes rivers overflow, flooding the surrounding areas almost completely and turning them into seas of water. But here and there, pieces of land will remain above water, providing animals with high ground where they can take sanctuary and survive the flood.

These floods represent the suffering and desires of human beings living in this world. Shakyamuni taught, "When we're drowning in the swirl of human desires and the sufferings we face in this world on earth, we must take refuge on the small island that is ourselves; this, and no other, is the shelter we must stand on. We always must rely on ourselves as we go through this life. After I die, there will come a flood tide carrying debris. But like the creatures that seek to take refuge on the sandbars that form, you must depend on yourself and protect your own haven. Rely upon yourself."

What Shakyamuni taught his disciples in these last moments on earth was a long way from a faith that abandons personal effort and trusts in other-power. He didn't teach his disciples to rely only on him to attain salvation after his death. Instead, he taught them, "Rely upon yourself, for each of you has Buddha-nature within your mind. Cherish its voice as you continue to live your lives."

In addition to teaching us to keep the torch within us lit, Shakyamuni Buddha also left behind the torch of dharma. He taught that after his death, we should live according to his teachings, because even as we relied upon ourselves, when it came to solving day-to-day problems, some situations may arise that we wouldn't know how to deal with. In these situations, we might wish to turn to our teacher for guidance, but he wouldn't be there, just as the full moon is sometimes hidden behind clouds. Shakyamuni taught that in these moments, we should base our decisions on the teachings that he'd left for us. Even in the last days of his eighty-year-long life, Shakyamuni emphasized living proactively by constantly refining the self, trusting the self, and observing the dharma as our guide.

3
Developing Oneness with Buddha

Buddhism teaches concepts such as the impermanence of all worldly things, the egolessness of all phenomena, and the perfect tranquility of nirvana. Some people may misunderstand these ideas, seeing them as negative and gloomy, and form an image of Buddhism as a religion of weakness. One Japanese psychologist* claimed, "Christianity is an aggressive religion, whereas Buddhism is passive. If you were to psychoanalyze Shakyamuni, you would discover that he had a weak personality."

People who think like this might interpret the teaching of the impermanence of all things to mean that everything is transient. Or they might think that the egolessness of all phenomena means that nothing in this world is substantial, so that neither they nor anyone else really exists. They may then conclude that Buddhists are pessimistic and nihilistic and refuse to go to school, are rarely seen at work, or never want to hold down a job. If

---

* Otoya Miyagi (1908–2005), a Japanese psychologist, author, and professor at the Tokyo Institute of Technology, is known for having introduced and popularized psychology in Japan.

this were true, it would be no wonder for people to regard Buddhism as a passive religion. But this interpretation of Buddhism is completely wrong.

When Shakyamuni saw that the eight decades of his life on earth and more than forty years of dedication to teaching and spreading the dharma were coming to a close, he taught his disciples, "Cherish your mind throughout your life. Always live according to the dharma. Do not depend on me, but rely on yourself, and be devoted to the Buddha within you." This shows that Buddhism is actually a very proactive religion.

Buddhism preaches a boundless trust in ourselves, in our own soul, and in the commitment to refining our soul. This continual effort to refine our soul is Buddhism's driving force. Buddha urges you to drive your ship forward using your own propellers.

The point I'm trying to make is that egolessness has nothing to do with the view that death will sweep away everything, and it has nothing to do with any lack of will or inner strength. On the contrary, Buddhism teaches us to develop a truly strong, radiant self that is one with Buddha. When you become truly one with Buddha, you will cease to be a weak human being of this world; instead you will be empowered by a strength previously unknown to you. You'll acquire the power of enlightenment, and that power will enable you to dissolve all your worldly suffering, pain, and attachments outright. A religion of such teachings as these is clearly a proactive religion.

Statues of Buddha are often accompanied by statues of Manjushri, the bodhisattva who represents wisdom and holds a sword called *the sharp sword of Manjushri*. This sword represents the power of wisdom to cut through all worldly manacles and attachments. It cuts away all obstacles on the path to enlightenment.

You can acquire this sharp sword of Manjushri through continuous spiritual training. You'll gain great power as you overcome various difficulties, discipline your mind, develop your inner strength, and abandon all sorts of worldly temptations and attachments. This power becomes like a spiritual sword that allows you to cut away any problems that may stand in your way. It's also the sword that quells evil. So not only is the sword able to cut away desires, attachments, and seductions; it can also conquer evil. This sword is also an oar you can use to ensure that you go in the right direction as you are carried downstream.

4
The Determining Factor for Heaven or Hell: Egolessness

My experiences of the other world have shown me how essential the teaching of egolessness is. Before I acquired my spiritual gifts, even if I had gained intellectual knowledge of the teaching of egolessness, I would have seen it simply as a recommendation to control my ego because over-assertiveness offends other people. But now, as someone who has experienced the world beyond this physical world, I cannot stress the importance of egolessness enough.

The world after death can be broadly classified into two realms: heaven and hell. I've met many souls who have fallen to hell, and I've listened to what they told me. All of them were experiencing suffering and pain. Whether they were aware of their own pain is another question, but their suffering was obvious to the ordinary person. They were suffering in a world full of destruction, violence, attachment, confusion, bewilderment, jealousy, envy, and warfare—malicious conflicts fought for the sake of satisfying greed. All the spirits in hell I've met were concerned only with themselves and sought only their own happiness, but they weren't able to escape from their suffering. And because they couldn't close the gap between their desire for happiness and the reality of their agony, their dissatisfaction only escalated. Then they blamed others and their environment for their misery. The more these spirits desperately sought to satisfy their desires, the more self-torment they brought upon themselves.

What's so sad about these spirits is that all they can do is think about themselves. All their ideas center on "me." If only they could abandon what they believe themselves to be, they could be happy, but they're unable to do so. What they think of as themselves is not the spiritual self. It's not the self that receives Buddha's Light, nor is it part of Buddha's Light. They identify with a "self" that has been strongly influenced and conditioned by this three-dimensional world. This is the "self" that has been molded by the environment in which they grew up, the education they received, old beliefs, and old patterns of thinking. They see only the "self" that is defined by their place of birth, family background, education, occupation, status, income, spouse, and so on, and can't bring themselves to let go of this "self."

I've heard spirits in hell insisting, "I am a government minister, so I cannot accept the way that I am being treated right now." "I am the president of a large corporation. Where is my driver?" These were truly dreadful scenes to witness. Another person was shouting, "I am the prime minister. Why am I being treated this way? You won't get away with this! Where is everyone else? Someone, come here, this instant!" All of them were too self-centered to understand what they were doing wrong.

In contrast to those living in hell, those in heaven are living in harmony. All of them truly care for one another. They live out their days extending love to one another, and they're happy. They refrain from trying to take love from others, and they practice kindness, fostering a community of happy, smiling people. In a higher realm, the realm of bodhisattvas, people are totally devoted to serving others' happiness. They are only concerned with giving. Ordinary people tend to think, "When I give, I lose something; when I receive, I gain." But there's something wrong with the basis of this kind of thinking.

In this material world, it's true that giving something away reduces the number of your possessions and receiving something increases the number of your possessions. For example, if someone gives you a thousand dollars, you'll gain that amount, while the person who gave it to you will lose the same amount. It seems to be the rule in the three-dimensional world that the person who gives something to others loses, while the person who receives this something gains.

But it works in the opposite way in the Spirit World. The more you give of yourself to others, the happier you are. The more you devote yourself to others, the more happiness you receive, because by giving of yourself, you're expanding yourself as a child of Buddha. When you give something, you become that much closer to Buddha, and you're able to radiate more of your light. Emanating this light as a child of Buddha enhances your happiness and expands your self. You experience yourself growing and becoming more like Buddha, and this gives rise to true happiness.

In short, happiness in the other world is a spiritual happiness that arises from growing in greater likeness to Buddha. The growth toward Buddha that we experience serves as our source of happiness in the other world. Take children, for example. Children take joy in seeing that they're growing year by year. They feel excited as they become taller and heavier, as their knowledge increases, and as they make friends at school. In the spirit world, too, you feel happy when you grow—not physically, but spiritually, as you approach Buddha, the source of all Light. Instead of growing heavier, you feel lighter, like the fresh breezes of May. To enjoy this feeling of lightness, you have to get rid of your attachment to "I," "me," and "mine."

Practicing love is a very important part of our spiritual training while we live on earth. We experience many types of love—the love between lovers, the love between husband and wife, the love between parent and child, and neighborly love. But there are two sides to these different shapes of love. Love can sometimes be used in the wrong way—that is, to bind others to yourself. So the love we express toward others can be gentle, but it can also be harsh; it's these two sides of love that create heaven and hell.

A parent's love for a child is not a love that expects any reward or recompense. But if a parent tries to bind a child, becoming greedy or possessive, or makes the child do things for him or her—in short, if a parent tries to use a child for his or her own ends—the parent's love may become wrong love, or what people in hell think of as love. So long as a parent gives love to a child without expecting any return, the child will be grateful and want to give back to the parent. But if the parent takes care of the child in hopes of getting something from the child in return, the parent is practicing taking love, and this will lead the child to rebel.

In this world, too, giving and taking love brings consequences similar to those in the other world. In this world, the giver is said to lose, while the person who receives is said to gain. But a business owner whose intention is to deliver quality merchandise to customers will ultimately prosper. On the other hand, someone who is always on the lookout for the slightest chance of making a profit and doesn't hesitate to cheat, take advantage of others, or deceive people will lose customers' trust in the end, even if the business seems successful at the outset.

When people can no longer survive in business, they're likely to start taking advantage of others. This type of person concentrates on depriving others.

A similar thing happens in religions. While some religious organizations work as hard as they can to bring happiness to large numbers of people, many pursue only worldly interests and seek to control others to satisfy their own greed. It may seem that many of these sorts of religions thrive in today's world. So it's important to see whether a religion is based on a willingness to give to others. You can tell whether a religion is leading people to heaven or hell by observing whether its founder and followers have a sincere desire to bring happiness to others or are only trying to satisfy their own desires for power and control.

Now you may understand why Shakyamuni Buddha taught the idea of egolessness again and again. His teachings on practicing a selfless perspective and not thinking of things as belonging to ourselves arose from his wish to help us save ourselves and prevent us from spreading a hell around us.

5
Advice on Egolessness

Egolessness Does Not Mean Suppressing Individuality

Practicing egolessness does not mean suppressing your individuality. When you become egoless, you don't become characterless. The practice of egolessness shouldn't result in a denial of our unique personalities or becoming bland like jelly; this would contradict the true will of Buddha.

Look at the wealth of different plant and animal species. Buddha appreciates the development and prosperity of the individuals that create the artistry of the world as a whole. He values highly the process by which we each contribute to the world he created in our own way based on the spirit of self-help. Intelligent people use their brains; robust people use their physical strength. All of us should contribute our individual light and participate in the creation of heaven on earth by doing what we can, a woman as a woman, a man as a man, a parent as a parent, a child as a child, and an elder as an elder. It's very important to respect each person's individuality.

Egolessness does not mean suppressing individuality. Expressing your individuality doesn't imply taking from or depriving others; instead it's a process of illuminating the world with your own unique light. Individuality is like a searchlight, a torch, or the light of a candle. There are many candles, and they burn with flames of different shapes and colors, but when each of those unique lights attempts to illuminate the world, an ideal world will emerge.

Don't Allow Other People's Egos to Become Inflated

I would now like to raise another point to bear in mind in relation to egolessness. Members of the *sangha*, or the spiritual community of our organization, have a mutual understanding based on Buddha's Truth. This shared understanding makes it possible for our members to create an ideal world by following the teachings of egolessness, restraining our desires, and living for the benefit of others. But we need to be aware that practicing egolessness could be harmful when we're among those who are still unaware of the Truth and haven't yet entered the world of the sangha. Our egoless attitude should not cause other people's egos to inflate, but occasionally this does seem to happen.

Those who understand Buddha's Truth can understand and give to one another. But to a person who has absolutely no knowledge of Buddha's Truth and thinks in a completely different way—in other words, in a way that leads to hell—those who do not have egos sometimes appear simpleminded and easy to deceive. A person who tries to take advantage of other people's egolessness is like a wolf among sheep.

As we practice egolessness, we should not mislead people who try to take advantage of us, who deceive or steal, so that their egos become inflated; that would be like pouring oil on fire. It's a matter of wisdom. If we're wise, we'll never try to add to the sum of suffering; instead, we'll try to reduce it. And if we're wise, we'll try never to add to the sum of human mistakes; instead we'll try to prevent mistakes. So if you wish to become wise, you must not encourage those who do wrong, who are already committing crimes or are about to, and add to their sins or bad karma. Instead you must stop them from making a mistake.

There are two ways to do this. First, you should always be on your guard so that your egolessness, your attitude of giving love as if you were in the heavenly world, does not encourage other people's wrong desires. When you're dealing with people who have a strongly egocentric mindset, you should keep a certain distance from them if you don't think it is the right time to invite them to join your group. Setting a wolf loose among a flock of sheep and saying "we are sheep" is not wise. You must be cautious and keep your distance from wolves. This attitude is not born of selfish desire, nor does it imply that you're preserving your ego. It's simply important to have this wisdom. Second, if you think a person is gradually awakening to the Truth, then you should offer adequate guidance little by little.

Avoid Self-Deprecation

Egolessness leads to humility and gratitude. But some people allow humility and gratitude to lead to self-deprecation. Beware of making this mistake; putting ourselves down or humiliating ourselves is not the same as egolessness. Some of us put ourselves down thinking that doing so will help us practice humility and gratitude, but this attitude only causes others to elevate their position relative to us. As a result, we may mistakenly cause others to look down on us and consequently cause them to become conceited. We must learn to distinguish the difference between "remaining humble" and "lacking inner strength."

Give with Wisdom

There is a risk of turning the idea of egolessness into a mistaken form of giving love that could lead to others' downfall. We must not lead others on with sugared words such as, "I can give you everything you want," which may lead them to overindulge. On the other hand, there's also a risk that our egoless attitude may be merely self-abasing, and a self-abasing attitude will dispirit us and encourage others to become egotists who lack self-reflection and humility.

Even though egolessness is associated with heaven, it can lead others in the wrong direction if we don't also practice wisdom. We must not put the idea of egolessness into practice in a way that will increase other people's wrongdoing or cause them to make new mistakes. This is where we need to apply wisdom. In this case, wisdom is like the sharp sword of Manjushri. It's important to put a stop to others' wrong desires, point out their errors, and avoid putting ourselves in the position of leading others in a wrong direction.

We need to be strong—not in a worldly sense on our own account, but as our true selves, who are of service to Buddha. What's most important is that we let the work of Buddha advance each day and be mindful not to apply our egolessness in a way that could disrupt the work of Buddha.

6

Egolessness and Love that Nurtures Others

To practice egolessness, we can begin by restraining our own ego and self-centered desires. Gluttonous pride, inordinate competitiveness, and disdain toward others are dreadful tendencies that need to be kept under self-control if we are to live in harmony with one another. We should also prevent people who haven't yet reached that level of self-control from going in the wrong direction. We shouldn't apply the idea of egolessness in a wrong way that will increase others' egotism; instead, we should use wisdom as a tool against wrong action. The stern guidance we offer when we point out what is wrong in someone's mistake is a form of love called nurturing love.

If we give love blindly, without wisdom, it may lead to others' downfall. This is why we must evolve our love to a higher level—to the level of nurturing love that guides others in the right direction. And to guide others properly, it's important to understand the difference between good and evil, because we need to know what's wrong to be able to choose what's right. Unless we have this ability, we won't know how to create what's good.

It's important to be able to recognize evil and choose not to get involved in it and to stay away from it, even if it's within easy grasp. By striving to do so, we're able to bring about goodness in this world.

We need to beware not to misunderstand egolessness: it doesn't mean being easily influenced by both good and evil. Being egoless means keeping yourself untainted, as if you were a clean, white cloth. It's easy for a white cloth to become stained, but being egoless doesn't make us susceptible to staining. A cloth can be washed if it becomes dirty. So, the constant effort we make to keep our cloth white represents our constant effort to do our best to increase the radiance within ourselves.

I hope this chapter has inspired you to think about how you can put egolessness into practice to improve yourself and society as a whole.

SIX

PRACTICING THE PHILOSOPHY OF THE MIDDLE WAY

1
Avoiding Extremes

I would now like to talk about practicing the Middle Way. The aim of this chapter is not just to explain the logic behind the philosophy of the Middle Way, but also to look at how we can practice this teaching in our everyday lives. Perhaps the phrase "Middle Way" evokes the image of taking the path of moderation, of not going to extremes—an impression we gain from the name itself. So we sometimes represent the Middle Way by pressing our palms together in prayer, which is generally believed to be the most harmonious image of the Middle Way. But when we think about practicing the Middle Way in our day-to-day lives, it may be hard to grasp what these extremes are actually referring to.

So I will start by explaining these extremes. The purpose of the concept of the Middle Way is, after all, the abandonment of suffering and the attainment of a peaceful state of mind. The extremes we need to avoid are conditions that cause us suffering—and the causes of this suffering are closely related to the condition of our bodies and our state of mind.

2

Blaming the Outside World and Blaming the Inner Self

First, let's take a close look at some problems of the mind that we often face. In what situations do you feel inner pain? For instance, two extreme cases might be when you place a lot of blame either on the outside world or on yourself.

What do we do when we blame the outside world? We blame other people or our surroundings for our distress and unhappiness. When we do this, our mind fills with hatred, anger, jealousy, envy, and suspicion. From the viewpoint of the invisible world of our mind, it will look as if our mind, eyes, and mouth are constantly sending arrows of criticism toward others. This is one extreme.

When we perceive everyone else as being in the wrong and can't stop criticizing, disparaging, and speaking ill of others, our mind becomes obsessed by the thought, "He is to blame," or "She is to blame," which then becomes a wellspring of critical thoughts toward others that we may also sometimes direct onto our environment or social circumstances. These are examples of feelings we have when we wish to find fault with the outside world.

Of course, our criticisms are sometimes valid; we may well be facing serious problems that other people are causing. In those cases, we need to use our wisdom to solve our difficulties.

When we look at the social conditions surrounding us recently, we see that we've been faced with sources of suffering such as natural disasters and economic recessions. You may wish to blame the earthquake, the tsunami, the forest fire, the flood, the drought, or the famine for your suffering. Maybe there was an oil shortage, your profession faced a downturn, or your whole industry is going under. In fact, there are many situations that you as an individual can't do anything about—some things are just beyond human control—so it's not always a mistake to recognize these kinds of situations as the causes of your suffering.

So at times, it's true that you suffer because of changes in your external conditions. But as you look at these outside factors, ask yourself whether you can change them through your own efforts. If you think you can, there's still room for you to make an effort. For example, imagine that you're a mother with young children. If your children do something wrong, you can chide them to encourage rectification, instead of simply complaining and worrying about their behavior. To regain peace of mind, you can choose to be proactive: you can point out their mistakes to your children and warn them not to repeat the same mistakes again.

However, in cases that involve the whole of society, things aren't as simple. In these situations you first need to realize that just worrying or complaining about other people or your environment is counterproductive. Next, ask yourself if there is anything you can do about the situation. Is there a way to use your own paddle to cross a torrent of pain and suffering and get back to the shore? Searching for something you can do to improve the situation in this way is more productive than endlessly listing your causes for complaint.

On the other hand, your mind may go in the direction of blaming, punishing, or tormenting yourself. This is the second of the two extremes, and this attitude is also wrong, because it may eventually cause you to doubt that you are a child of Buddha. As I have said over and over again, no matter how miserable your conditions are and no matter how much pain and sorrow you're experiencing, Buddha is constantly pouring out His great love into each of you. Even if, right now, you're suffering in a deep chasm of agony, warm eyes are still watching over you. Sometimes people are judged good or bad as a result of their thoughts and deeds. You may even find yourself labeled "bad." But Buddha keeps on pouring the light of the sun and the rain of compassion upon every person, regardless of whether they are good or have made a mistake.

When you feel truly grateful for the great compassion of Buddha and come to realize the true worth of your own being, you may make the decision to transform, improve, and reflect on yourself to correct your shortcomings. This is a very positive and commendable mindset. But if you're too hard on yourself and start becoming self-deprecating, saying or thinking, "I'm good for nothing," you could become discouraged and negative. You may then try to win the sympathy of others, become obsessed by an inferiority complex, have difficulty trusting others, avoid meeting people, and in the end live like a hermit, still dissatisfied and grumbling. This is certainly a state to be avoided.

Whereas the first extreme, blaming outside factors, is aggressive, the second extreme seems from an outsider's point of view to be passive and negative about oneself. Although self-reflection is important, we must not dwell on the pitch-black wrongs we may notice about ourselves, but instead focus on our true self-worth. Some people who have been raised in Christian environments have difficulty getting away from the idea that human beings are born sinful; they consider their origins to be completely evil. There are also groups of people who see themselves as children of Satan and believe that satanic blood is flowing through their veins. This is a sad situation, because that belief diminishes their chances of finding happiness, and it's not at all the truth.

As we've seen, there are two extremes: an attitude of aggressive attack toward the outside world and a tendency to deprecate oneself, even sometimes to the extent of driving oneself to spiritual suicide. Neither way can lead to true happiness. The Middle Way is the state of mind that avoids both these extremes. I would like you to remember this as a way of controlling your mind in everyday life.

In short, you must not attribute too much of your happiness or unhappiness to outside factors and, at the same time, you must not blame yourself for unhappiness to the extent that you destroy yourself or deny your Buddha-nature or divine nature, for neither of these attitudes will serve your happiness in life.

3

The Middle Way Lets You Manifest Your Buddha-Nature

Human beings have an essential divine nature, or Buddha-nature, within. It's the diamond at the core of our minds, and it can also be understood as the nature that makes it possible for us to attain enlightenment. We are such precious beings. But on earth, we live in a physical body, controlled by the six sense organs—the eyes, the ears, the nose, the tongue, the tactile body, and the consciousness—and we're influenced by other people's opinions, our social circumstances, our educational background, and our work environment. As we live our lives under these conditions, our views gradually become distorted, which eventually leads to suffering. The root of our suffering lies in mistaken thoughts and actions that originate in what we've absorbed from this world.

Although it's important not to forget that you are a being of great value, you also need to remember that the cause of suffering is to be found in your own thoughts and actions. You are basically a good, blessed being, but you create suffering for yourself when your thinking or your actions are mistaken.

But when you avoid clinging to any extreme, you'll reach the state of mind known as the Middle Way. This is a harmonious state that harms neither yourself nor others, and this is the state of mind that can help us create utopia on earth. Trying to deny who you are or criticizing others unnecessarily doesn't lead to happiness in the end. But holding the wish to live in harmony with others does lead to realizing utopia on earth and is also the practice of the Middle Way.

What kind of attitudes of mind can we gain through the Middle Way? We can cultivate consideration for others, modesty, kindness, thoughtfulness, the willingness to make an effort, gratitude, and faith. The Middle Way is also characterized by a loving and harmonious heart—a heart that feels gratitude toward others, leads you to cooperate with them, and keeps you humble. In addition, as you live in this physical world on earth, your mind gradually becomes covered over with unwanted "rust." So, along with practicing these attitudes of mind, every day, you also need to practice removing this rust from your mind. When you do these things on a daily basis, you'll harm neither yourself nor others. This practice is what I think self-reflection is.

Practicing self-reflection requires a humble attitude. Looking humbly at your mistakes enables you to set them right. Without a sense of humility, the six worldly delusions—greed, anger, foolishness, pride, doubt, and false views—will wreak havoc upon your mind. You can free yourself from these delusions if you can restore your true self as a child of Buddha. If you can't honestly see yourself as the child of Buddha that you really are, all sorts of desires and suffering will arise in your mind. You'll be carried away by your own greed or by other people's opinions and evaluations. You'll gradually lose sight of your true self, and this loss will become the source of the suffering you experience in life.

4
Finding Balance between Body and Spirit

So far, I have explained the Middle Way from a spiritual perspective. Now, let me proceed to another important point in the practice of the Middle Way, which is to find balance between our body and spirit. This is actually the most important point of all.

There is an extreme philosophy that asserts that we human beings are only flesh and that we live in a world that consists only of matter. This view is materialistic and values only the material world. On the other hand, there are people who are excessively absorbed in the Buddhist philosophy of the *void* or *emptiness* and who deny the things of this world completely. Although they have a religious disposition, they're so eager to abandon this world that they fall into the trap of nihilism. If everyone were to become like this, this world could never become like heaven. Instead, hell would unfold. If people thought of nothing but how to escape from this world, it would never become an ideal world.

Although the spirit world really does exist, it's not right to completely deny the meaning of this earthly world or to try and ignore it. Materialistic views and spiritual views are two extremes, but neither can be avoided completely as long as we live in this world. For this reason it's all the more important to seek a balanced view of both and strive to harmonize our body and spirit.

In Buddhism, the phrase "mind and matter are one" expresses this balance. This means that the body and the spirit cannot be completely separated. Let's look into this further. I once read a book written by a Japanese Zen master, the self-appointed successor to the Buddhist scholar Daisetsu Suzuki (1870–1966 CE). According to this Zen master, because the body and mind are one, when the body perishes, the mind perishes too. In short, he says that when a body is cremated, the mind also vanishes into thin air. But this view is the equivalent of the idea that everything comes to an end when we die. And that is one of the false views that Shakyamuni Buddha disapproved of. It seems that the Zen master did not understand this for two reasons: he himself was unable to recognize spiritual beings, and he didn't have faith in Buddha. He devoted himself solely to physical training based on a materialistic perspective and, as a result, ended up with a miserably shallow level of enlightenment. I would like you to remember that extreme views on the relationship between the body and the mind actually do exist.*

* Ryomin Akizuki (1921–1999 CE), a Japanese Buddhist scholar and author, wrote about his disbelief in the existence of the soul, the other world, reincarnation, and the law of causality and asserted the mistaken view that Buddhism is based on atheistic, materialistic perspectives and denies the existence of any Divine Being or spiritual existences.

5

Cultivating a Spiritual Perspective: Practicing Self-Reflection

As you continue in your efforts to improve yourself and remove the unwanted rust from your mind, you'll begin to receive the Light of Buddha and guidance from your guardian and guiding spirits. Having reached this level, you will truly know that there is an infinite world beyond this third dimension.

Then you'll realize that your brother and sister souls have been constantly watching over you since you were born into this world, even though you may have thought you were undergoing your spiritual discipline alone. You may have had good thoughts and bad thoughts, but whenever you did something wrong, your spiritual brothers and sisters were watching over you from a distant world with tears in their eyes.

You'll realize that a spiritual being has been watching over you all this time. This spirit is not completely separate from you; it's your true self who is within you—your authentic self, a purity of heart that lies in your subconscious. Your guardian spirit represents this purity of heart and has been watching over you. Actually, the pure heart within you has constantly been watching over you as you've undergone your spiritual discipline in this three-dimensional world.

Usually, the subconscious lies hidden beneath the surface consciousness. While you're awake, your surface consciousness is active, from the time you wake in the morning till you go to bed at night. Your surface consciousness is not completely independent of the workings of your brain, your nervous system, and your other physical organs—they all interact with one another. Consequently, your surface consciousness is very susceptible to third-dimensional, materialistic vibrations and is easily influenced by other people. Although your surface consciousness is part of your mind, it's easily affected by the vibrations of this world on earth.

Imagine a crystal-clear lake. When autumn comes and leaves fall, the lake's surface becomes covered with leaves and other debris and looks messy. Although the water is clear, the surface does not look clean. This resembles the surface consciousness of a person living in this world of matter and undergoing spiritual discipline. One time in autumn, I stayed at an inn high up in the mountains; nearby there was a small stream. In the morning, I awoke to a rustling sound. Wondering what the noise was, I looked down from my window and saw the innkeeper raking up the fallen leaves that had collected on top of the stream. Until he swept the leaves away, I couldn't see the clear stream below.

This story is one way of explaining the meaning of the self-reflection that I constantly recommend. Although the surface consciousness is connected to the subconscious, it becomes covered over by worldly thoughts, clouding your ability to see the truth. Your guardian spirit is always watching over you, wanting you to hear his or her true voice, but if your surface consciousness is still muddled or cloudy, your guardian spirit will have difficulty reaching you.

As the clouds over your surface consciousness are cleared away, one at a time, through self-reflection, communication with your subconscious will become easier. What will happen then? You will be connected to heaven, even though you still live in a physical body. Your thoughts will coincide with the thoughts of your guardian spirit. This means you'll be able to see things from the viewpoint of heaven. As you live from a spiritual perspective, your own problems and worries will gradually disappear.

In this age, most people worry constantly about making decisions—what to do; which alternative to choose; when to do something; whether to do it now, tomorrow, or in a year; and so on. But when you are attuned to your guardian spirit, you can answer these questions from your guardian spirit's perspective, and you may find that your desires were misleading you. If you want to make a decision about changing jobs, getting married, or a business matter, your guardian spirit can give you the inspiration to make the decision that is best for your life. However, if your worldly desires or your attachment to the things of this world are too strong, you'll make wrong decisions and choose a wrong direction.

6
Knowing How to Be Content in Life

I have said that self-reflection is important. So what do we need to do to clear our surface consciousness and stay connected to our subconscious? One essential attitude is knowing how to be content.

While we live in this world on earth, it's not so easy to control our desires and stop them from increasing. We want more and more things. We may become arrogant. When we find ourselves in this sort of state, it's a good idea to reflect on ourselves, focusing on how we can be content. "I've been allowed to live today. I didn't die of starvation. Although many things happened, I managed to live one day, the Earth didn't disintegrate, the sun didn't stop shining, and I didn't lack food. I may have had various problems and worries, but I lived through today. There have been many days before this, and there will almost certainly be a tomorrow."

Reflect in this way and feel thankful that you are blessed with each day. Instead of aiming too high, love your life as it is now. You may not be totally satisfied with your present situation if you compare it to someone else's, but there's no telling whether the person you envy is truly satisfied. Each person has his or her own problems to face, and some of the people you hold in low regard may actually be leading wonderful lives.

Each of us leads our own life. Knowing how to be content means loving your unique life and embracing it. The desire for material things knows no end, and the same is true of the desire for money, the desire for status, the desire for fame, and the desire for sex. If a married couple who love each other raise a family and live in harmony for some decades, they're actually living the Middle Way, knowing how to be content. On the other hand, there's no end to the number of people you see who never learn how to be content, who indulge in extramarital affairs and destroy their families. They're well aware of what will happen if they behave in this way, but they're unable to control their desires, and as a result their family is destroyed.

It takes nearly thirty years for a couple to raise children, so it's extremely important to maintain the stability of the family for thirty years. If this stability is destroyed, the children's future will be affected and the parents' lives may also stray in the wrong direction. I would like to stress that to prevent a family from breaking up, it's essential to know how to be content.

In the India of Shakyamuni Buddha's day, disciples weren't allowed to have families of their own. Today, even religious professionals and practitioners have families of their own, so conditions for practicing the Middle Way are much more favorable than they were in the past. Religious professionals and lay people alike are allowed to have families and lead ordinary lives; each day can be valuable and precious. To keep a marriage from breaking up, a husband and a wife need to be thankful and appreciate one another's good points day in and day out, finding happiness in bringing up their children together. Looking for another man or woman who has the qualities your spouse doesn't have will never lead to true happiness.

Knowing how to be content is, in truth, the key to achieving life's greatest happiness. I would like you to remember that the way to ensure domestic happiness in these times is to know how to be content and to live according to the Middle Way. On the foundations of a secure family life, business life flourishes. In business, you may not always be as successful as others. You may feel inferior to someone you admire or consider a role model. But you should ask yourself what the purpose of your spiritual training in this lifetime is—what your assignment is. Then be determined to do the very best you can to solve the problems assigned to you in this lifetime.

I also recommend this way of thinking: "In the next life, I'll undergo a different kind of spiritual development, but in this life I was born into this environment and chose this job. It may be difficult to change my job completely, so I'll achieve as much as I can with what I have in this lifetime." It's no use for a farmer to envy a fisherman or for a fisherman to envy a farmer. When you're determined to achieve the best possible results from your spiritual development in this lifetime in your present occupation, the way to true progress and prosperity will open up.

If you live the Middle Way and know how to be content, you can avoid coming under negative spiritual influences. Always be on your guard, and you'll escape possession by the stray spirits that roam the streets and gather around misleading religions. Even if you are told that the cause of your sufferings is your ancestors who are still not able to return to heaven, if you live in harmony on earth, they won't have the chance to disturb you.* They'll see the harmonious life that you, their descendant, lead, and they'll reflect on themselves with tears of repentance. In this way, their situation will also improve.

Your first step on the Middle Way is to know how to be content to protect your mind from evil. Next, fill your home with the light of harmony to prevent evil or stray spirits from invading your family. It's greed that leaves you unguarded. Quarrels and strong, uncontrollable desires

---

* Ancestor worship is popular in Japan and other Buddhist countries, and people perform ritual services for their ancestors. In Buddhism, there is an idea that people can save those who passed away before knowing the Truth, and a ritual service for ancestors is believed to be one way of saving them. However, some misguided religions take this opportunity to threaten people, putting all the blame for their misfortune on their ancestors. This gives rise to many problems.

invite evil spirits to attack, so determine to always control your desires and walk the Middle Way together with your family. Be on your guard against evil; never let it enter your home. This is the path that promises you happiness for all eternity; it is the path of spiritual development that you should walk each day with steady steps.

SEVEN

ENLIGHTENMENT AND SPIRITUAL POWERS

1
Spiritual Experiences as a Precondition for Enlightenment

The main topic of this chapter is the relationship between enlightenment and spiritual powers. To begin with, I feel it's necessary to look back at my own experiences. In my case, there is no denying that my religious awakening was part of my mission even before I was born into this world and that my spiritual leanings contributed to it. But I have to say that my spiritual gifts and the spiritual experiences that led me to cultivate my spiritual powers were also essential factors that led to my enlightenment.

For some people, it's easy to accept religious Truth without experiencing doubt; it's enough simply to accept what they read or hear. But for me, my level of spiritual awakening and awareness changed completely after I actually experienced the existence of spiritual beings. To know that the spirit world really did exist came as a great surprise, even though I already had an intellectual understanding of it.

2
The Influence of Spiritual Experiences on Enlightenment

1. Knowing that the Spirit World and Eternal Life Are Real

An awareness of the spirit world influences enlightenment in stages. First of all, spiritual experiences open our eyes to the other world that lies beyond this three-dimensional, phenomenal world. This is already a huge leap. We human beings are born into physical bodies, grow old, and eventually die, but if we awaken to the reality that the soul, or spiritual self, continues to exist even after death, this realization will inevitably change the way we live now and in the future.

This is exactly what happened to me. I already had an intellectual understanding of the other world and reincarnation, but it was a great surprise to experience the existence of the spirit world firsthand and discover that the spiritual beings in that world retained the same ways of thinking and characteristics as they had while they were alive. It was also a great joy to realize that no effort we make in this world is ever wasted.

If we simply died without a trace at the age of seventy or eighty, what would be the purpose of making an effort our whole lives? Why should we seek goodness? Why should we pursue happiness? I don't think we could find answers to these questions. But when we know that we live on after death, we come to realize that what the religions, philosophies, and moralities of many different countries around the world have taught for thousands of years is the real truth. We start to understand that this life is only a period of transition until the next life. The soul is born into this world like a caterpillar that goes into a chrysalis, and the soul returns to the other world just as the caterpillar eventually turns into a butterfly, leaving its chrysalis behind. We realize that reincarnation is like a metamorphosis: what was once a caterpillar in a past life enters a chrysalis in this lifetime and becomes a butterfly in the next life. From a spiritual viewpoint, this three-dimensional world is full of restrictions but is like a period when a butterfly remains in a chrysalis, in deep contemplation. So knowing that the spirit world exists is certainly a great leap toward enlightenment.

2. Understanding Good and Evil in the Real World

However, simply becoming aware of the existence of the other world does not mean that you have attained enlightenment. As you accumulate more spiritual experiences, an undeniable truth will unfold before you. You'll come to know that both heaven and hell truly exist in the world after death and that there are both good and bad spirits. The existence of the spirits in heaven and hell may come as a great surprise or even a shock to you.

When you contact spiritual beings directly, you'll learn that heaven and hell, good spirits and bad spirits, are divided based on completely different standards from the ones we value in this world. You will be surprised to see how few people in this world know this truth. People who pursue only earthly values are highly likely to fall to hell and become stray spirits after they die. For many people, when they realize this, they know they're in deep trouble.

The thing that surprised me most was seeing that some people who had had social status, wealth, position, and intelligence while they had lived on earth had gone to hell and become stray spirits. When I saw them creeping away to escape the agonies of hell, possessing people still living on earth, and ruining the lives of the people they possessed, I could not believe that they had once been human and had seemed refined. Meanwhile, I saw other people who had not been well off or accomplished in this world and were now enjoying a wonderfully abundant happiness and joy and total freedom in the other world as a result of their wholehearted and diligent efforts to refine their minds. I was impressed to see that such great happiness really exists.

So, the second stage of enlightenment is learning what good and evil are through direct contact with the spirit world. Without this spiritual experience—without knowing the solemn reality that heaven and hell do exist—it would be very difficult to know what good and evil really are. When you gain this understanding of good and evil, you'll be able to clearly distinguish good spirits from bad and heaven from hell. Then you'll be able to see whether your current state of mind is closer to heaven or to hell and anticipate which direction you're likely to head after death. If you can understand this, you've reached an important stage on the path to enlightenment.

To summarize, the first stage of enlightenment is knowing that life is eternal and that the other world actually exists. The next stage is understanding that both good and evil exist in the other world, that there is a clear distinction between them, and that you'll be evaluated according to your thoughts and actions during your life on earth. Knowing this is the second great leap toward enlightenment.

3. The Diversity of the Spirit World Reflects the Diversity of Life on Earth

The third stage of enlightenment is learning how diverse and hierarchical the states of the human mind can be. Hell is not a simple place; there are as many different varieties of hell as there are tendencies of the human mind. You would understand this if I described the characteristics of each and every hell that exists. But there are too many to describe here, so let me tell you about a few to give you a sense of their variety.

Souls who have fallen to the Hell of Villains used to be aggressive, constantly harassing, cursing, and slandering others. If you saw how they constantly torment one another in the same way, you'd understand why they ended up there. Souls who are wriggling in the Hell of Lust or the Hell of the Bloody Pond were always obsessed by lust, filled with sexual desires, and entangled in immoral affairs. You would see that obsession with lust is a living hell. Those who abandon human dignity, never respected spirituality, and followed materialistic desires and animal instincts will go to the Hell of Beasts when they die. When you see these people living just like animals, in both appearance and behavior, it's hard to hold back the tears. But their appearance is an exact reflection of the desires they clung to while they were living in this world. When their souls break free from the constraints of the physical body and express themselves freely, they transform themselves into animals; their various appearances are manifestations of their unconscious desires. Seeing this shocking reality would terrify you.

These days, people who advocate atheism and materialism may pass for smart intellectuals; in fact many are active in the media. But there's a clear distinction between, on one hand, intellectuals who, whether or not they're conscious of it, believe in the spiritual world and live in accordance with their faith and, on the other hand, those who promote materialistic views such as "God doesn't exist," "Physical material is the only reality," and "Humans are no different from machines." The latter type will fall to Abysmal Hell and spend day after day crying out in agony along with the souls of those who led large numbers of people astray by imbuing them with wrong ideas. Seeing all these souls suffering in hell reminds us that when we eventually return to the other world, we'll be rewarded and punished for the good and evil we do in this world. Everything comes back to how we live in this world. Everyone has a key that opens the door to all possibilities.

Heaven is also made up of various worlds on different levels: the Astral Realm (the fourth dimension), the Goodness Realm (the fifth dimension), and the Light Realm (the sixth dimension); the Light Realm is where highly intellectual divine spirits live. Higher still is the Bodhisattva Realm, or spirits filled with love and compassion (the seventh dimension), and the Tathagata Realm, the great leaders (the eighth dimension). If you would like to know Buddha, you will be able to sense His existence as you ascend to higher and higher levels in the spirit world. Heaven is indeed vast.

Imagine what great happiness a soul enjoys as it strives for eternal spiritual refinement in the heavenly world. In the physical world, you have to graduate from school, but there's no graduation from schools in the spirit world. Once you finish a course, the next one awaits you. This eternal process of advancement gives rise to feelings of great joy. Feelings of light and beauty always accompany this joy. While the world of true enlightenment is filled with happiness and joy, hell is filled with sorrow, despair, and agony. You'd be appalled if you knew just how big the gap between the state of heaven and the state of hell is.*

If you've been reading my books and listening to my lectures, you should be able to reach the first stage of enlightenment, the stage of accepting that the spirit world exists and that human beings have eternal life. It's also possible to attain the second stage of enlightenment, which is understanding the existence of heaven and hell,

* People create their own life plans before they're born, but some are overwhelmed by the negative influences of the material world in the third dimension, give themselves over to physical desires, and end up in hell when they die. But they can earn the chance to restart their lives if they reflect on and repent their wrong thoughts and deeds. Spirits in hell cannot be born on earth until they've repented for their mistakes and risen to at least the Posthumous Realm in the fourth dimension.

the distinction between good and evil, and the spiritual values that separate them and applying these values to yourself. The third stage of enlightenment is grasping the hierarchy and diversity of the spirit world. In this stage, you know that the spirit world's many levels correspond precisely to the diverse thoughts and actions of people living in this world. If you can understand this, you've already attained quite a high level of enlightenment for a human being still living in this world on earth.

4. Acquiring Wisdom in the Physical World

So, what is the fourth stage of enlightenment? As long as you live in this world on earth, you can't break away from the limitation of living in a physical body. When you die and return to the spirit world, you may well become a high-level spirit and free yourself from all physical restrictions, but in this world, you're bound by the conditions of the third dimension. As long as you live here, you can't escape problems and worries. Day by day, week by week, month by month, and year by year, you're constantly confronted by problems. And to restore your tranquility of heart and peace of mind, you need to solve these problems.

Even if you possess innate spiritual powers or have become spiritually aware, you won't be able to receive guidance or inspirations from divine spirits as long as your heart is assailed with worries. A distressed heart inevitably attracts stray spirits, so it's important to resolve any problems that are causing you distress. To do this, you need to acquire wisdom, which is one of the most important objectives of living in the three-dimensional world.

As long as we're living in this three-dimensional world, we can't live in exactly the same way as the inhabitants of the spirit world do. In heaven, people live in harmony; they have none of the troubles or worries that lead to hell. But earth is replete with obstacles to leading a heavenly life, and we can't avoid encountering negative spirits and lost souls from hell. Directly or indirectly through other people, we all eventually come into contact with negative spiritual influences of hell. And this contact often brings worries along with it.

How can we solve the problems and anxieties that cause us distress? By acquiring wisdom. And we can acquire wisdom by gaining the knowledge of the Truth. By practicing what we've learned, we can back up our knowledge with experience. In this way, we can develop and strengthen our wisdom. With the wisdom we acquire, we'll be able to resolve our problems as decisively and swiftly as if we're using the sharp sword of Manjushri. The sword of Manjushri represents the power of wisdom, and with this power, we'll be able to cut through any worries we may face. All sorts of attachments may arise from within, one after another. But with the power of wisdom, we'll always be able to get rid of them so we can maintain a tranquil heart and a state of emancipation.

3
The Relationship between Enlightenment and Spiritual Power

Enlightenment and spiritual power are very closely related; in fact, they can't be separated. However, there are many psychics who aren't enlightened enough to realize that they're being manipulated and controlled by negative spiritual influences. I would call these psychics "spiritually disturbed" rather than "spiritually gifted," because they're constantly possessed by malicious spirits and behave as these spirits dictate. You can easily tell whether psychics have come under negative spiritual influences by examining their behavior. In most cases, those who lead aberrant lifestyles are controlled by evil spirits. Those who are always behaving in eccentric or outlandish ways to attract attention are also attuned to spirits in hell.

Many typical psychics start their own spiritual groups, and a simple way to find out which ones have come under negative spiritual influences is to look at the desires they express. For example, if you can tell that a spiritual leader is only interested in taking love from others, that leader has come under negative spiritual influences. If someone is always thinking about taking from others, that mindset will instantly tune in to a realm in hell.

Although spiritual power is necessary to grasp the spirit world, it's also an extremely unreliable ability in this three-dimensional world, where we're always vulnerable to material values. So even if you've acquired spiritual power, you need to remind yourself daily to lead a disciplined life, harmonize your mind, and constantly strive to avoid becoming conceited or arrogant; otherwise your mind will easily attune to hell. For this reason, it is important to take precautions against this pitfall and make diligent efforts each day.

Unfortunately, there is no denying that more than 90 percent of those who claim to be psychic have come under negative spiritual influences. I would like you to know that spiritual power alone does not lead to enlightenment, although this ability or the knowledge obtained through this ability is essential to the attainment of enlightenment.

4

Enlightenment through Faith: The Bridge-Building Theory

You may wonder whether ordinary people who do not have spiritual power can ever attain enlightenment. It's true that without direct spiritual experience, it's difficult to grasp the existence of the Spirit World. But there is a theory that makes it possible. Even if you don't have direct experience, you can still build a bridge and cross over it to the world of enlightenment by having faith in those who have grasped the truth of the Spirit World and attained enlightenment using their spiritual gifts. Even if it is not your own direct experience, you can still experience enlightenment through faith, and safely, too. Enlightenment through faith will offer your soul safety and peace of mind in the physical world and, at the same time, can give you the same sort of power as if you had actually attained enlightenment yourself.

What can we attain as a result of enlightenment through faith? The basic prerequisite for enlightenment is to live in the right way so you can avoid going to hell after death. And for this, it is important to overcome problems and anxieties and lead a peaceful life while still in this world. The path to enlightenment means finding peace in this world as well as in the other world while aiming for the constant advancement of the soul. This being the case, we can achieve similar results from enlightenment through faith as we gain from achieving enlightenment directly.

5
A Long Way from Enlightenment: The Zen Sect

Of all the sects of Buddhism, Zen may be the one that many people most closely associate with enlightenment. But when I look at nearly two thousand years of history and examine the level of enlightenment of Zen Buddhism, I must say that very few of even the most famous Zen priests actually attained enlightenment.

Based on the Truth taught at Happy Science, almost none of the Zen priests truly attained enlightenment. For example, the Japanese Zen priest Sojun Ikkyu (1394–1481 CE) is well known in Japan through anecdotes that reveal his sense of humor. Although he is still respected today as a quick-minded Zen priest, a close examination of his life clearly indicates that he was provoked by malicious spirits. He was a waggish Zen priest who was always eccentric and was influenced by villain spirits.

There is a tendency in Zen Buddhism to think that the enlightened should behave bizarrely like Ikkyu, who may appear to have been witty and eccentric. But this is a serious mistake; that kind of life is not the goal of religious discipline. Unfortunately, the Zen sect doesn't have the insight to understand this crucial error.

I would like to point out another mistake the Zen sect makes—one that has to do with its promotion of sitting meditation. Zen practitioners have reduced meditation to mere physical disciplines; they pursue sitting cross-legged but neglect true spirituality. In other words, their meditation is atheistic and materialistic. Zen seekers know little about spirituality; they believe that people can develop their willpower and meditative powers just by meditating cross-legged every day. They think of enlightenment as a sort of willpower to be obtained through continual physical discipline. But if you have studied the Truth taught at our organization, you will understand that the mere pursuit of willpower and physical strength does not lead to a higher level of enlightenment.

Among Zen seekers are some who attempt to attain enlightenment through intellectual investigation alone. But intellectual discipline alone can't bring enlightenment either. The main reason that the direction of the Zen sect has diverged so far from enlightenment is that none of the leaders had profound spiritual experiences. Their seeking was just sitting in meditation and working on Zen koans, the short sentences that aim to bring students to a greater awareness of reality through contemplation.

In contrast, T'ien-t'ai Chih-i (538–597 CE), a Chinese Buddhist monk and philosopher who had spiritual experiences and great intellectual knowledge, attained quite a high level of enlightenment. In fact, he understood firsthand the secret of the inner world, which is that thoughts can attune to all the many realms of the spirit world.

6
What Is True Enlightenment?

Enlightenment is truly difficult to attain. Even if you become capable of communicating with the spirit world, you don't automatically attain enlightenment. On the other hand, if you completely neglect the spirit world and pursue the formal practice of meditation merely as a physical discipline, you're also a long way from enlightenment. If you think you can attain enlightenment simply by repeatedly contemplating the nonsense and incomprehensible riddles posed by Zen dialogues with the aim of defying the values of this world, you are also a long way from the world of truth.

In the world of truth and enlightenment, great ideas prevail. There you will find orderly systems of principles and ideas. Love, compassion, courage, harmony, and wisdom—these wondrous ideals that apply in this physical world also apply in the world of truth. This is the reality of the world of enlightenment.

Today's religions, including Buddhism, are extremely confused because they no longer understand the world of enlightenment. But true enlightenment must not only be based on a knowledge of the spirit world, but also show people living on earth how to improve themselves steadily and constantly to ensure a peaceful life after death.

In this chapter, I have discussed the subject of enlightenment and spiritual powers. Some of you may wish to attain enlightenment by acquiring spiritual powers. However, your life is not limited to just this one lifetime. Each of you has experienced numerous lifetimes, and through these experiences you have formed a particular karma—particular soul tendencies. Your tendencies might manifest as a mission to show others what enlightenment is by drawing on your own direct spiritual experiences. But if this doesn't happen to you, instead of merely pursuing spiritual powers, determine to build a bridge with faith and walk steadily to the shore of enlightenment. Now that the path to true enlightenment is paved before you, I believe it would be a great decision for you to follow this path.

EIGHT

WHAT IS KARMA?

1

Good Karma and Bad Karma

The theme of this chapter is karma, an idea that may sound rather old-fashioned but that embraces an eternal Truth that is neither old nor new. This Truth relates to you yourself in the present moment.

According to Buddhism, karma is more or less synonymous with *action*, because karma is generated by actions. For action to occur, *will* must be at work. Your own will—your intention to do something—manifests as physical movement. At that moment, your thought and action are permanently etched on the record of your life. So karma is created and shaped by our intentions and actions.

Naturally, there is both good karma and bad karma, since there are both good actions and bad ones. However, karma often has negative implications because it is closely related to the system of reincarnation. Before we are born into this world, we prepare a rough plan of the life we are going to live on earth. The more advanced the soul, the more complex and detailed the life design is. Souls at lower spiritual levels tend to draw less sophisticated life plans. In any case, once you are born, you inevitably experience all sorts of difficulties in this three-dimensional world. Faced with such difficulties, you may think they are the outcome of karma from your past lives. When you attribute your difficulties, tragedies, pain, sadness, and distress to past-life karma, you will naturally see karma as inherently negative.

But there is a pitfall in this human way of thinking. If you look back at your whole life, you can't possibly claim that it has constantly been miserable, as if it rained the whole time. If you recall your life as an endless series of unhappy experiences, one after another, that's probably just your way of remembering things. When you look back over your life carefully and objectively, as if you were watching scenes of your entire life projected on a movie screen, you will surely see that you've had both ups and downs. In fact, unfortunate events are frequently preceded by happy times.

Happiness and unhappiness arise as the cumulative results of the various experiences you've had. On the last day of your life, when you look back, it will be up to you to decide whether you lived a happy life or an unhappy one. If you think you've lived an unhappy life, you are probably recalling only the miserable experiences. On the other hand, if you think you've lived a happy life, you are recalling a lot of the good times, although you've probably experienced bad times as well. So it's a matter of which aspects of your life you focus on.

If you engrave a tragic event very sharply on your soul, this memory may linger for decades. For example, you may become a victim of a natural disaster. If you were nearly buried or killed by a landslide but had a narrow escape, you might not be able to free yourself from this nightmare even after twenty or thirty years. That traumatic memory might leave a lasting mark on your life, making you think that you've lived your whole life in unhappiness. But it all depends on which images you choose to hold in your mind.

2
Ignorance Causes Bad Karma

You may wonder whether it's possible for karma to last through the past, present and future. The answer is yes, but only to a certain degree. While you can't carry your physical body with you through the cycle of reincarnation, you can take your mind, which is the core part of your soul. What you engraved on your mind when you lived in this three-dimensional world in the past will greatly influence your life now. If you have the kind of mentality that attracts unhappiness, you will often experience misfortune. In contrast, if you develop a keen sense of happiness or are receptive to happiness, you're more likely to encounter a lot of happy events. These sorts of inclinations can be likened to different tastes in food. You probably have certain likes and dislikes when it comes to food. You may prefer plain tastes to rich tastes; you may prefer Japanese dishes to Italian. You may not know why you like or dislike certain foods, but you still have your own set of preferences. Similarly, your soul has acquired particular likes and dislikes. As a result of numerous past incarnations, you've developed certain tastes or senses of the soul that have become your tendencies and preferences. And strangely enough, many people prefer unhappiness to happiness.

You may find it too simplistic to attribute such choices to the inclinations or preferences of your soul. But the reason you make bad choices is actually ignorance, or spiritual darkness, which is described in Buddhism as the first of the twelve links of causality that explain the suffering of human beings.* Ignorance means lacking the light of wisdom. With the light of wisdom illuminating our path, we can walk without danger, whereas if we grope around in the dark, we may trip and fall, which often happens to many people.

We all live unique lives in our own way, but if a wiser person were placed in the same situations we've faced, he or she would not make the mistakes we made. For example, children are safe if their parents are by their side, keeping an eye on them, but if they're left by themselves, they may fall and get hurt. This happens because children usually can't foresee danger. Even among adults, there are big differences in levels of knowledge, experience, and insight. We may be able to avoid failures if someone with deeper insight gives us good advice. Or others may be

* The twelve links of causality is a Buddhist concept that describes the cause of suffering and the course of events that leads human beings to go through birth, aging, and death. The twelve links are ignorance, action, consciousness, name and form, six sense organs, contact, feeling, craving, grasping, existence, birth, and aging and death. For a more detailed explanation, see chapter 6 of *The Challenge of Enlightenment.*

able to easily handle a particular situation that's difficult for us to deal with. Looking at these examples, we see that ignorance is not an absolute state, but rather a relative state. Depending on our particular circumstances—which involve many factors, such as ability, personal relationships, financial situation, living environment, and family relationships—we may find it extremely difficult to handle certain challenges. And it's in these situations that we often cannot avoid failure.

3
Wisdom Crushes Ignorance

What should we do to crush our ignorance and turn it into wisdom? If we stay the way we are, we'll naturally keep making choices according to the particular tendencies of our souls. So it's essential to get rid of those inclinations—and the best way to do this is to respect the views and suggestions of people who have more insight than we have. Let's return to the example of the child who can avoid getting hurt if accompanied by a grown-up. From a spiritual perspective, the adult's perspective is equivalent to the advice of our guardian and guiding spirits. In worldly terms, without going into the spiritual aspects, this means mastering the knowledge of the Truth or the teachings about Buddha's Will.

One of the reasons I always recommend learning the Truth is that this knowledge can help you stay out of trouble. Many people find themselves in difficult situations simply because they don't know the Truth. Imagine an old, open well in the ground. If you know where the well is, then you know that it's dangerous to go near it. But if you don't know about it, you can easily fall into it. The old well is a metaphor for the materialistic views of the many people who live dissolutely, thinking, "There is nothing after death," or "There is no such thing as the afterworld." These sorts of people are unaware of the danger that lies in front of them while they're indulging in pleasure. Consequently, they fall into the well.

Warning people about the old well is like letting them know that hell really does exist. It's like telling them to watch how they live, because there's a danger that they could fall into hell. It's like saying, "You're living in this physical world now, but there's another world where you'll go after you die. If you live in the wrong way, you'll suffer in your next life. So live carefully." To warn people of this danger, our organization offers books of the Truth and holds lectures and seminars. And if you can maintain a peaceful state of mind, you may receive your guardian spirit's inspiration and guidance to avoid these pitfalls.

Based on my readings of people's lives and numerous past incarnations, I can confirm that each person has particular soul tendencies, which allows me to predict, to some extent, how they'll react and behave when they face issues in their workbook of life. What I predict often matches the way they end up acting. They behave in certain ways, as if their souls lure them into particular actions. So if you'd like to overcome your tendencies, you need to step out of the framework of your own way of thinking and acquire a higher level of awareness.

The same holds true in the world of business and management. When confronted with a crisis, a person with strong managerial capability can easily overcome it, while a less capable person can easily bring the company to bankruptcy. It's often said that only one in five entrepreneurs succeeds at starting and running a business. In most cases, failure is caused not by the environment or bad luck, but by their lack of ability and managerial skills. You can't depend on someone else to teach you how to manage your business. You'll need to master this ability by studying, thinking, and taking action. Managerial ability is something that you need to acquire on your own, and it's not something that you can easily learn from someone else. A great many companies go bankrupt every year as a result of the management's lack of skills and experiences. Many of these bankruptcies could be prevented if they could get help from good consultants or advice from someone with stronger managerial skills.

In fact, many people are capable in a worldly sense, but viewed from a higher level of insight or from a spiritual point of view, these intelligent people may be spiritually ignorant. Even someone who seems to have excellent skills and the highest levels of intelligence may know next to nothing from the viewpoint of the high-level spirits in the other world. From the higher perspective of heaven, people living in the three-dimensional world are like ants in a miniature garden inside a box. The ants may be proud of their expert knowledge of the miniature garden, but they don't realize that they're captives in a small box. People who take pride in their worldly abilities are like ants that are proud of their thorough knowledge of their miniature garden. These ants are certainly cleverer than ants that lack such knowledge. They may even be able to use their knowledge to avoid potential dangers. This analogy shows the true state of people living in the three-dimensional world.

4
Mistaken Beliefs about Ritual Services for the Dead

As I explained above, karma is formed by the choices you make according to the tendencies of your mind and the actions you take on the basis of your judgments. Karma will remain on the record of your life; it's an inclination of the mind that will also influence your future incarnations.

We must consider the current activities of different religious groups in light of this truth. Not only new religious organizations, but also traditional groups often use the term "karma" in a way that implies only negative karma. Many of them claim that the karma of your ancestors, grandparents, parents, siblings, and so on will bring you misfortune, so you must get rid of it. They then say that you must participate in their ritual service to sever your ties with your relatives' karma. But no matter how much you pay for such a service, it won't have much effect if it's based on mistaken beliefs.*

---

* See the footnote about ancestor worship in chapter 6, section 6.

One religious group claims that people can suffer from various karmas, such as the karma of imprisonment, the karma of lust, and the karma of accidental death. According to their theory, your ancestor's karma of imprisonment will cause you to go to jail. If your ancestors were involved in tangled love triangles and had problems in sexual relations, that makes you prone to the karma of lust, so you won't be able to live a happy life until you get rid of that karma. If you're under the influence of your ancestors' karma of accidental death, the same fate will befall you. This religious group persistently exhorts its followers to buy a model pagoda or a rosary to pray for their ancestors or pay for a ritual service to get rid of their ominous karma.

Many new religious groups in Japan engage in similar practices. Their theories vary, but they all say that we must get rid of the karma of our ancestors and deceased family members. One group offers "karma talk," in which followers talk about their ancestors' ominous karma and then urge people to buy dubious objects to erase their sins. This is a common trick that religious groups ridden with evil spirits use to deceive people.

5

Good Religions Teach Self-Reflection and Self-Responsibility

It's very possible that among the members of your family, there is a soul who has not been able to return to heaven, whether it's your father or mother, a grandparent, or someone from a previous generation. If you trace your family lineage all the way back, at some point, you'll probably find a soul that hasn't been able to return to heaven. So in theory, it is possible that the soul of an ancestor could be influencing his or her descendants.

A certain religious group takes advantage of this theory to justify its practice of performing daily rituals for its followers' ancestors. This may be one way to get rid of negative spiritual influences from the dead. I teach that negative spiritual influences may sometimes affect your health or your decisions in a negative way and cause you to suffer. But I also teach that you can cut yourself off from such negative vibrations by disciplining your mind, correcting your actions, and harmonizing your thoughts. I've also said that if you live a righteous and harmonious life, you can set an example for ancestors who may be suffering in the other world because they lived wrongly on earth. They may be able to save themselves by following your example.

Let me explain this with an analogy. Suppose a father is burdened with a huge debt and his son is burdened with an equally huge debt of his own. Is it possible for the son to pay off his father's debt when he himself is in debt? The answer is no. But if the son is a successful and wealthy businessman, then can he clear his father's debt? The answer is yes. The relationship between ancestors and descendants is exactly the same as the relationship between the father and son. Souls who have failed to return to heaven are like people who suffer under a heavy burden of debt. These souls suffer on account of the "spiritual debts" they incurred during their lives on earth.

Even if a descendant wants to clear an ancestor's spiritual debt so the ancestor can return to heaven, if the descendant is living a corrupt life and is also under negative spiritual influence, he or she may also be in debt spiritually. One person in debt can't pay off another person's debt. To clear someone else's debt, you need sufficient savings. Only if you've built wealth can you pay off another person's debt. "Wealth" in a spiritual sense is the virtue you've built up during your life on earth, and you accumulate this wealth through your daily spiritual training based on the teachings of the Truth. The virtue of the light of Truth is your heavenly wealth, and only if you've accumulated this kind of wealth can you offer light to others and share it with people in trouble.

This is the right way of thinking when offering services for ancestors. Simply offering amulets or any other ritual implements won't save lost souls. Instead, it's essential that their descendants or those with ties with them accumulate virtue every day. When we practice right religious disciplines, we receive light from our guardian and guiding spirits. So if we pray for our ancestors' happiness while practicing these disciplines, we can pay off their "debts" using the "assets" of our virtue.

Some people may decide to hold services for their ancestors because they want to free themselves from agonizing conflicts, struggles, and suffering, such as illness, financial difficulties, or entangled relationships. They may think, "My misery must be the fault of my ancestors. Their curse is causing my suffering. So if I can drive them away, I should be able to live happily." In reality, these people not only fail to drive away the lost souls of their ancestors but also descend into the world of darkness themselves. We should stay on guard and be careful not to fall victim to the unscrupulous practices of misguided religions that prey on people's vulnerability.

Suppose someone told you that you have the karma of imprisonment because one of your ancestors went to prison. But if you had to go to prison, it would be because you broke the law; your ancestor wouldn't be responsible for the crime you committed. Claiming that you were imprisoned because of your ancestor's karma of imprisonment is simply irresponsible. Similarly, if you were to blame a car accident entirely on the curse of an ancestor's karma, saying, "I ran over someone because my ancestor once committed a murder," you're simply denying your fault. Or suppose you committed a crime of passion as a result of the complications of a love affair. It would be nonsense to say, "This is the curse of my ancestor's karma of lust, so it's not my fault. It happened because my ancestor hasn't returned to heaven. All I need to do is hold a ritual service for the repose of my ancestor's soul." You'd be not only denying your responsibility for controlling your own mind and actions, but also failing to repent your wrongdoing.

So, you can tell that a religion is wrong if it blames the bad karma of your ancestors or deceased family members for any bad things that happen to you, because that means that it denies self-responsibility and repentance for any wrongdoing. Such a religion may even extort large sums of money for getting rid of bad karma. This kind of religion has fallen victim to evil spirits and is completely controlled by spirits in hell.

What distinguishes a good religion from a bad one is whether it properly teaches self-reflection and self-responsibility to those who are living now and undergoing spiritual discipline in this world. I would like you to use this point as a guideline if you come across religious groups that offer ritual services for ancestors. Religious groups that invariably blame your ancestors for everything, saying, "It's your ancestors' fault that you're unhappy" or "You can only be happy if your ancestors were virtuous" are quite wrong. We ourselves create our own happiness and unhappiness, and the main mission of religion is to save those who are living in this world now.

6
A Shared Destiny: Group Karma

Although karma is essentially about taking responsibility for our individual lives, we also share a common destiny with the rest of our society and the whole of the human race. When a large-scale war breaks out, a fate befalls us that we can't escape, no matter how rightly we're living. This shared fate is referred to as "group karma," as opposed to the "individual karma" of each person.

Upon hearing this, some people may complain, "You say we shouldn't blame our misfortunes on our environment, society, or the times we live in, but now you're telling us we have group karma. If an outbreak of a war forces me to kill the enemy against my will, what do you have to say about that?" or "Why do I have to suffer in an economic recession even though I work very hard to run my own business?" What you need to remember in this case is that human beings cannot live alone. We can't live in solitude on a desert island like Robinson Crusoe. We're all part of a community, and we're closely linked with one another by endless chains of cause and effect. This means that you are at least partially responsible if your society isn't functioning properly. While you should place great importance on your own spiritual development, you should also always have a desire to help create a better world as a member of your community, society, or country.

To dispel the negative tendencies of our group karma, we need to increase the number of our fellow humans who spread light. To do this, we should convey the Truth to as many people as possible, speaking to each and every person with sincerity and enthusiasm. In this way, we can prevent our common destiny and group karma from heading in the wrong direction. Now that many catastrophic phenomena are occurring, it's essential for each one of us to correct and refine our own mind. But it's an equally essential spiritual practice to let people know that when each and every person pursues Right Mind, and when this movement spreads to the whole, we can change the course of our shared destiny.

To conclude, truly good religion should teach its followers that benefiting the self should benefit others, which means that we should pursue our own spiritual growth while at the same time guiding others to walk the right path. I hope this chapter helps you deepen your understanding of this essential point.

AFTERWORD

This book, *The Challenge of the Mind*, is the third volume in the "challenge" series, preceded by *The Challenge of Religion* and *The Challenge of Enlightenment*. The purpose of Buddhism was not to teach how to preserve coelacanths, which are "living fossils," or train monks as cemetery administrators. Rather, the aim of this religious philosophy was to encourage you to challenge your mind and break through the bounds of religions' potential.

I have imbued old Buddhist philosophy with new life, and these new teachings now brim with an intellectual, logical, and positive, challenging spirit. I will establish this new philosophy to take the place of outdated teachings. I hope that my easy-to-understand explanations will lead old, misguided religious ideas to their final end.

Religion should now be restored to the hands of the true elite—the Light of Bodhisattvas. The leap of progress that Happy Science fulfills will, indeed, mark the official coming of the age of these spiritual elites.

Ryuho Okawa
Founder & CEO
Happy Science Group

ABOUT THE AUTHOR

Founder and CEO of Happy Science Group.

Ryuho Okawa was born on July 7th 1956, in Tokushima, Japan. After graduating from the University of Tokyo with a law degree, he joined a Tokyo-based trading company. While working at its New York headquarters, he studied international finance at the Graduate Center of the City University of New York. In 1981, he attained Great Enlightenment and became aware that he is El Cantare with a mission to bring salvation to all humankind.

In 1986, he established Happy Science. It now has members in 169 countries across the world, with more than 700 branches and temples as well as 10,000 missionary houses around the world.

He has given over 3,500 lectures (of which more than 150 are in English) and published over 3,150 books (of which more than 600 are Spiritual Interview Series), and many of which are translated into 42 languages. Along with *The Laws of the Sun* and *The Laws of Hell*, many of the books have become best sellers or million sellers. To date, Happy Science has produced 27 movies under his supervision. He has given the original story and concept and is also the Executive Producer. He has also composed music and written lyrics of over 450 pieces.

Moreover, he is the Founder of Happy Science University and Happy Science Academy (Junior and Senior High School), Founder and President of the Happiness Realization Party, Founder and Honorary Headmaster of Happy Science Institute of Government and Management, Founder of IRH Press Co., Ltd., and the Chairperson of NEW STAR PRODUCTION Co., Ltd. and ARI Production Co., Ltd.

BOOKS BY RYUHO OKAWA

The Laws of the Sun

One Source, One Planet, One People

Paperback • 288 pages • $15.95
ISBN: 978-1-942125-43-3 (Oct. 25, 2018)

Imagine if you could ask God why he created this world and what spiritual laws he used to shape us—and everything around us. Ryuho Okawa outlines these laws of the universe and provides a road map for living one's life with greater purpose and meaning. This powerful book shows the way to realize true happiness—a happiness that continues from this world through the other.

The Laws of Eternity

El Cantare Unveils the Structure of the Spirit World

Paperback • 224 pages • $17.95
ISBN: 978-1-958655-16-0 (May 15, 2024)

"Where do we come from and where do we go after death?" The other world has a multidimensional structure consisting of the worlds of the fourth, fifth, sixth, seventh, eighth, and ninth dimensions, where souls with the same level of spiritual awareness and similar characteristics reside. Encountering the long-hidden Eternal Truth that are revealed for the first time in human history will change the way you live your life now.

Latest Laws Series

The Laws of Hell

"IT" follows.....

Paperback • 264 pages • $17.95
ISBN: 978-1-958655-04-7 (May 1, 2023)

Whether you believe it or not, the Spirit World and hell do exist, and unfortunately, 1 in 2 people are falling to hell. To stop hell from spreading and to save the souls of all human beings, Ryuho Okawa has compiled vital teachings in this book. This publication marks his 3,100th book and is the one and only comprehensive Truth about the modern hell.

The Laws Of Messiah

From Love to Love

Paperback • 248 pages • $16.95
ISBN: 978-1-942125-90-7 (Jan. 31, 2022)

"What is Messiah?" This book carries an important message of love and guidance to people living now from the Modern-Day Messiah or the Modern-Day Savior. It also reveals the secret of Shambhala, the spiritual center of Earth, as well as the truth that this spiritual center is currently in danger of perishing and what we can do to protect this sacred place.

The Laws of Secret

Awaken to This New World and Change Your Life

Paperback • 248 pages • $22.95
ISBN:978-1-943869-99-2 (Apr. 20, 2021)

Our physical world coexists with the multi-dimensional spirit world and we are constantly interacting with some kind of spiritual energy, whether positive or negative, without consciously realizing it. This book reveals how our lives are affected by invisible influences, including the spiritual reasons behind influenza, the novel coronavirus infection, and other illnesses.

Other Books

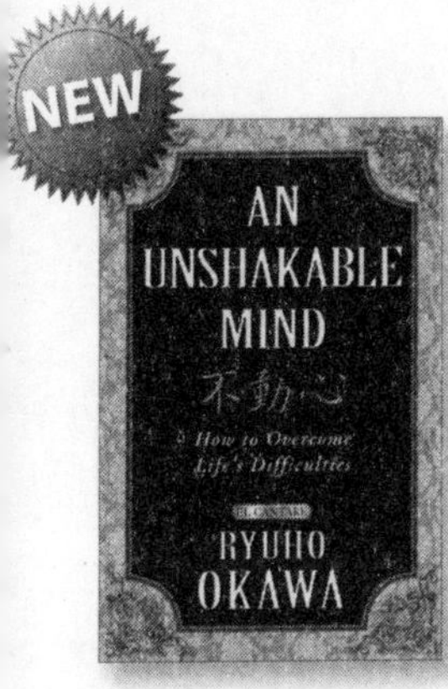

An Unshakable Mind

How to Overcome Life's Difficulties

Paperback • 180 pages • $17.95
ISBN:978-1-942125-91-4 (Nov. 30, 2023)

This book will guide you to build the genuine self-confidence necessary to shape a resilient character and withstand life's turbulence. Author Ryuho Okawa breaks down the cause of life's difficulties and provides solutions to overcome them from the spiritual viewpoint of life based on the laws of the mind.

The Essence of Buddha

The Path to Enlightenment

Paperback • 208 pages • $14.95
ISBN: 978-1-942125-06-8 (Oct. 1, 2016)

The essence of Shakyamuni Buddha's original teachings of the mind are explained in simple language: how to attain inner happiness, the wisdom to conquer ego, and the path to enlightenment for people in the contemporary era. It is a way of life that anyone can practice to achieve lifelong self-growth.

The Rebirth of Buddha

My Eternal Disciples, Hear My Words

Paperback • 280 pages • $17.95
ISBN: 978-1-942125-95-2 (Jul. 15, 2022)

These are the messages of Buddha who has returned to this modern age as promised to his eternal beloved disciples. They are in simple words and poetic style, yet contain profound messages. Once you start reading these passages, you will remember why you chose to be born in the same era as Buddha. Listen to the voices of your Eternal Master and awaken to your calling.

Words of Wisdom Series

Words for Life

Paperback • 136 pages • $15.95
ISBN: 979-8-88737-089-7 (Mar. 16, 2023)

Ryuho Okawa has written over 3,150 books on various topics. To help readers find the teachings that are beneficial for them out of the extensive teachings, the author has written 100 phrases and put them together. Inside you will find words of wisdom that will help you improve your mindset and lead you to live a meaningful and happy life.

Words for Building Character

Paperback • 140 pages • $15.95
ISBN: 979-8-88737-091-0 (Jun. 21, 2023)

When your life comes to an end, what you can bring with you to the other world is your enlightenment, in other words, the character that you build in this lifetime. If you can read, relish, and truly understand the meaning of these religious phrases, you will be able to attain happiness that transcends this world and the next.

Words to Read in Times of Illness

Hardcover • 136 pages • $17.95
ISBN: 978-1-958655-07-8 (Sep. 15, 2023)

Ryuho Okawa has written 100 Healing Messages to comfort the souls of those going through any illness. When we are ill, it is an ideal time for us to contemplate recent and past events, as well as our relationship with people around us. It is a chance for us to take inventory of our emotions and thoughts.

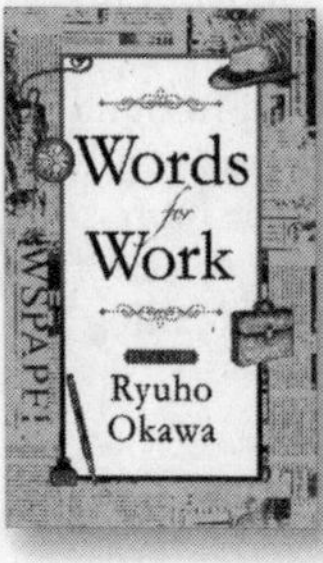

Words for Work

Paperback • 140 pages • $15.95
ISBN: 979-8-88737-090-3 (Jul. 20, 2023)

Through his personal experiences at work, Okawa has created these phrases regarding philosophies and practical wisdom about work. This book will be of great use to you throughout your career. Every day you can contemplate and gain tips on how to better your work as well as to deepen your insight into company management.

Other Recommended Titles

THE UNHAPPINESS SYNDROME
28 Habits of Unhappy People (and How to Change Them)

THE TRUE EIGHTFOLD PATH
Guideposts for Self-Innovation

THE MIRACLE OF MEDITATION
Opening Your Life to Peace, Joy, and the Power Within

THE TEN PRINCIPLES FROM EL CANTARE VOLUME I
Ryuho Okawa's First Lectures on His Basic Teachings

THE TEN PRINCIPLES FROM EL CANTARE VOLUME II
Ryuho Okawa's First Lectures on His Wish to Save the World

TWICEBORN
My Early Thoughts that Revealed My True Mission

THE LAWS OF HAPPINESS
My Miraculous Story of Overcoming Illness and DeathLove, Wisdom, Self-Reflection and Progress

SPIRITUAL WORLD 101
A Guide to a Spiritually Happy Life

THE POWER OF BASICS
Introduction to Modern Zen Life of Calm, Spirituality and Success

---

For a complete list of books, visit okawabooks.com

WHO IS EL CANTARE?

El Cantare means "the Light of the Earth." He is the Supreme God of the Earth who has been guiding humankind since the beginning of Genesis, and He is the Creator of the universe. He is whom Jesus called Father and Muhammad called Allah, and is *Ame-no-Mioya-Gami*, Japanese Father God. Different parts of El Cantare's core consciousness have descended to Earth in the past, once as Alpha and another as Elohim. His branch spirits, such as Shakyamuni Buddha and Hermes, have descended to Earth many times and helped to flourish many civilizations. To unite various religions and to integrate various fields of study in order to build a new civilization on Earth, a part of the core consciousness has descended to Earth as Master Ryuho Okawa.

Alpha is a part of the core consciousness of El Cantare who descended to Earth around 330 million years ago. Alpha preached Earth's Truths to harmonize and unify Earth-born humans and space people who came from other planets.

Elohim is a part of the core consciousness of El Cantare who descended to Earth around 150 million years ago. He gave wisdom, mainly on the differences of light and darkness, good and evil.

Ame-no-Mioya-Gami (Japanese Father God) is the Creator God and the Father God who appears in the ancient literature, *Hotsuma Tsutae*. It is believed that He descended on the foothills of Mt. Fuji about 30,000 years ago and built the Fuji dynasty, which is the root of the Japanese civilization. With justice as the central pillar, Ame-no-Mioya-Gami's teachings spread to ancient civilizations of other countries in the world.

Shakyamuni Buddha was born as a prince into the Shakya Clan in India around 2,600 years ago. When he was 29 years old, he renounced the world and sought enlightenment. He later attained Great Enlightenment and founded Buddhism.

Hermes is one of the 12 Olympian gods in Greek mythology, but the spiritual Truth is that he taught the teachings of love and progress around 4,300 years ago that became the origin of the current Western civilization. He is a hero that truly existed.

Ophealis was born in Greece around 6,500 years ago and was the leader who took an expedition to as far as Egypt. He is the God of miracles, prosperity, and arts, and is known as Osiris in the Egyptian mythology.

Rient Arl Croud was born as a king of the ancient Incan Empire around 7,000 years ago and taught about the mysteries of the mind. In the heavenly world, he is responsible for the interactions that take place between various planets.

Thoth was an almighty leader who built the golden age of the Atlantic civilization around 12,000 years ago. In the Egyptian mythology, he is known as God Thoth.

Ra Mu was a leader who built the golden age of the civilization of Mu around 17,000 years ago. As a religious leader and a politician, he ruled by uniting religion and politics.

ABOUT HAPPY SCIENCE

Happy Science is a religious group founded on the faith in El Cantare who is the God of the Earth, and the Creator of the universe. The essence of human beings is the soul that was created by God, and we all are children of God. God is our true parent, so in our souls we have a fundamental desire to "believe in God, love God, and get closer to God." And, we can get closer to God by living with God's Will as our own. In Happy Science, we call this the "Exploration of Right Mind." More specifically, it means to practice the Fourfold Path, which consists of "Love, Wisdom, Self-Reflection, and Progress."

Love: Love means "love that gives," or mercy. God hopes for the happiness of all people. Therefore, living with God's Will as our own means to start by practicing "love that gives."

Wisdom: God's love is boundless. It is important to learn various Truths in order to understand the heart of God.

Self-Reflection: Once you learn the heart of God and the difference between His mind and yours, you should strive to bring your own mind closer to the mind of God—that process is called self-reflection. Self-reflection also includes meditation and prayer.

Progress: Since God hopes for the happiness of all people, you should also make progress in your love, and make an effort to realize utopia in which everyone in your society, country, and eventually all humankind can become happy.

As we practice this Fourfold Path, our souls will advance toward God step by step. That is when we can attain real happiness—our souls' desire to get closer to God comes true.

In Happy Science, we conduct activities to make ourselves happy through belief in Lord El Cantare, and to spread this faith to the world and bring happiness to all. We welcome you to join our activities!

We hold events and activities to help you practice the Fourfold Path at our branches, temples, missionary centers and missionary houses

Love: We hold various volunteering activities. Our members conduct missionary work together as the greatest practice of love.

Wisdom: We offer our comprehensive books collection, many of which bookstores do not have available. In addition, we give out numerous opportunities such as seminars or book clubs to learn the Truth.

Self-Reflection: We offer opportunities to polish your mind through self-reflection, meditation, and prayer. There are many cases in which members have experienced improvement in their human relationships by changing their own minds.

Progress: We also offer seminars to enhance your power of influence. Because it is also important to do well at work to make society better, we hold seminars to improve your work and management skills.

CONTACT INFORMATION

Happy Science is a worldwide organization with branches and temples around the globe. For a comprehensive list, visit the worldwide directory at happy-science.org. The following are some of our main Happy Science locations:

United States and Canada

New York
79 Franklin St., New York, NY 10013, USA
Phone: 1-212-343-7972
Fax: 1-212-343-7973
Email: ny@happy-science.org
Website: happyscience-usa.org

New Jersey
66 Hudson St., #2R, Hoboken, NJ 07030, USA
Phone: 1-201-313-0127
Email: nj@happy-science.org
Website: happyscience-usa.org

Chicago
2300 Barrington Rd., Suite #400,
Hoffman Estates, IL 60169, USA
Phone: 1-630-937-3077
Email: chicago@happy-science.org
Website: happyscience-usa.org

Florida
5208 8th St., Zephyrhills, FL 33542, USA
Phone: 1-813-715-0000
Fax: 1-813-715-0010
Email: florida@happy-science.org
Website: happyscience-usa.org

Atlanta
1874 Piedmont Ave., NE Suite 360-C
Atlanta, GA 30324, USA
Phone: 1-404-892-7770
Email: atlanta@happy-science.org
Website: happyscience-usa.org

San Francisco
525 Clinton St.
Redwood City, CA 94062, USA
Phone & Fax: 1-650-363-2777
Email: sf@happy-science.org
Website: happyscience-usa.org

Los Angeles
1590 E. Del Mar Blvd., Pasadena,
CA 91106, USA
Phone: 1-626-395-7775
Fax: 1-626-395-7776
Email: la@happy-science.org
Website: happyscience-usa.org

Orange County
16541 Gothard St. Suite 104
Huntington Beach, CA 92647
Phone: 1-714-659-1501
Email: oc@happy-science.org
Website: happyscience-usa.org

San Diego
7841 Balboa Ave. Suite #202
San Diego, CA 92111, USA
Phone: 1-626-395-7775
Fax: 1-626-395-7776
E-mail: sandiego@happy-science.org
Website: happyscience-usa.org

Hawaii
Phone: 1-808-591-9772
Fax: 1-808-591-9776
Email: hi@happy-science.org
Website: happyscience-usa.org

Kauai
3343 Kanakolu Street, Suite 5
Lihue, HI 96766, USA
Phone: 1-808-822-7007
Fax: 1-808-822-6007
Email: kauai-hi@happy-science.org
Website: happyscience-usa.org

Toronto
845 The Queensway
Etobicoke, ON M8Z 1N6, Canada
Phone: 1-416-901-3747
Email: toronto@happy-science.org
Website: happy-science.ca

Vancouver
#201-2607 East 49th Avenue,
Vancouver, BC, V5S 1J9, Canada
Phone: 1-604-437-7735
Fax: 1-604-437-7764
Email: vancouver@happy-science.org
Website: happy-science.ca

INTERNATIONAL

Tokyo
1-6-7 Togoshi, Shinagawa,
Tokyo, 142-0041, Japan
Phone: 81-3-6384-5770
Fax: 81-3-6384-5776
Email: tokyo@happy-science.org
Website: happy-science.org

London
3 Margaret St.
London, W1W 8RE United Kingdom
Phone: 44-20-7323-9255
Fax: 44-20-7323-9344
Email: eu@happy-science.org
Website: www.happyscience-uk.org

Sydney
516 Pacific Highway, Lane Cove North,
2066 NSW, Australia
Phone: 61-2-9411-2877
Fax: 61-2-9411-2822
Email: sydney@happy-science.org

Sao Paulo
Rua. Domingos de Morais 1154,
Vila Mariana, Sao Paulo SP
CEP 04010-100, Brazil
Phone: 55-11-5088-3800
Email: sp@happy-science.org
Website: happyscience.com.br

Jundiai
Rua Congo, 447, Jd. Bonfiglioli
Jundiai-CEP, 13207-340, Brazil
Phone: 55-11-4587-5952
Email: jundiai@happy-science.org

Seoul
74, Sadang-ro 27-gil,
Dongjak-gu, Seoul, Korea
Phone: 82-2-3478-8777
Fax: 82-2-3478-9777
Email: korea@happy-science.org

Taipei
No. 89, Lane 155, Dunhua N. Road,
Songshan District, Taipei City 105, Taiwan
Phone: 886-2-2719-9377
Fax: 886-2-2719-5570
Email: taiwan@happy-science.org

Taichung
No. 146, Minzu Rd., Central Dist.,
Taichung City 400001, Taiwan
Phone: 886-4-22233777
Email: taichung@happy-science.org

Kuala Lumpur
No 22A, Block 2, Jalil Link Jalan Jalil Jaya
2, Bukit Jalil 57000,
Kuala Lumpur, Malaysia
Phone: 60-3-8998-7877
Fax: 60-3-8998-7977
Email: malaysia@happy-science.org
Website: happyscience.org.my

Kathmandu
Kathmandu Metropolitan City,
Ward No. 15, Ring Road, Kimdol,
Sitapaila Kathmandu, Nepal
Phone: 977-1-537-2931
Email: nepal@happy-science.org

Kampala
Plot 877 Rubaga Road, Kampala
P.O. Box 34130 Kampala, UGANDA
Email: uganda@happy-science.org

ABOUT IRH PRESS USA INC.

Founded in 2013, New York based IRH Press USA Inc. is the North American affiliate of IRH Press Co., Ltd., Japan. The Press exclusively publishes comprehensive titles on Spiritual Truth, religious enrichment, Buddhism, personal growth, and contemporary commentary by Ryuho Okawa, the author of more than 3,150 unique publications, with hundreds of millions of copies sold worldwide. For more information, visit Okawabooks.com.

Follow us on:

- Facebook: Okawa Books
- Youtube: Okawa Books
- Pinterest: Okawa Books
- Instagram: OkawaBooks
- Twitter: Okawa Books
- Goodreads: Ryuho Okawa

NEWSLETTER

To receive book related news, promotions and events, please subscribe to our newsletter below.

irhpress.com/pages/subscribe

AUDIO / VISUAL MEDIA

YOUTUBE

PODCAST

Introduction of Ryuho Okawa's titles; topics ranging from self-help, current affairs, spirituality, religion, and the universe.